# AN OCCUPATION IN CONFLICT

*A Study of the Personnel Manager*

# AN OCCUPATION IN CONFLICT

## A Study of the Personnel Manager

*By* GEORGE RITZER

*Assistant Professor of Sociology,*
*Tulane University*

AND

## HARRISON M. TRICE

*Professor of Industrial and Labor Relations,*
*Cornell University*

New York State School of Industrial and Labor Relations
*A Statutory College of the State University at*
Cornell University, Ithaca, New York

1969

Library of Congress Catalog Card Number: 76-627591
SBN 87546-033-3

Price: $5.00 cloth

ORDER FROM

Distribution Center, New York State School
of Industrial and Labor Relations,
Cornell University, Ithaca, N. Y. 14850

PRINTED IN THE UNITED STATES OF AMERICA BY
W. F. HUMPHREY PRESS INC., NEW YORK

# Preface

AS THE field of personnel management has grown in importance, the occupation most commonly called "personnel manager" has proliferated. The growth of a subfield of sociology devoted to the study of occupations has paralleled the rise of the personnel manager. This study of the personnel manager has taken a hard look at several concepts developed in occupational sociology in order to understand better the emerging status of the personnel manager.

This study had its beginning in the fall of 1963 when graduate students in Professor Trice's courses in Organizational Behavior and in Personnel Management started systematic observations of personnel managers "in their native habitat." Sixty personnel managers were interviewed and observed as they engaged in a wide array of "situations faced." From these initial data grew many of the basic premises explored in the present study. One question raised was: to what extent do personnel managers fit the traditional image given them by textbook writers and professors? Also, some of the elements of a professional trend were detected and the conflict potential in the role was noted.

The study reported in this monograph began in late 1966 when the American Society for Personnel Administration met with representatives of the New York State School of Industrial and Labor Relations at Cornell University. Chief ASPA representatives included President Robert Berra, Executive Vice-President Leonard Brice, and Vice-President Frank Plasha. Principal Cornell people at these initial meetings were Dean David Moore, Dean Robert Risley, and Professor Trice. ASPA was interested in having Cornell undertake a large-scale study of its membership, to be followed by an extensive training program. ASPA is a nationwide association with a membership of approximately 4,500 of which over half (2,410) are personnel managers. Therefore, the study focused primarily on them.

Because of his long-standing interest in the occupation, Professor Trice agreed to conduct the study. George Ritzer was appointed research associate to supervise the project. Data were gathered by means of a nationwide questionnaire and a series of in-depth interviews. Susan Gottesmann and Nelson Olmedillo joined the project soon after its inception as research assistants. As the research progressed a number of other persons were engaged in various aspects of the project, including: over-all consultant, James Belasco; statistical consultants, Jack Arbuthnot and John Turney; computer consultants, Tom Armstrong and Marilyn Schell; coder, Susan Ritzer; and typists, Diane Emerson, Patricia Smith, and Elizabeth Greene. Diane Emerson acted as general secretary to the project.

The major part of the project consisted of a sixteen-page questionnaire which took a year to develop. It went through a number of pretests, which included over a hundred pretest interviews and a mail pretest. In order to supplement the questionnaire data, seventy-five research interviews were conducted with personnel managers. All of this was done by the four principal researchers — Professor Trice, Miss Gottesmann, and Messrs. Ritzer and Olmedillo. Although it is difficult to separate the specific contributions of each person in a large-scale collective effort, certain credits can be allotted. Professor Trice acted as director and over-all supervisor, and contributed to conceptualization, data analysis and interpretation, and to manuscript writing. George Ritzer carried the major responsibility for originating and coordinating basic theoretical concepts, especially in the area of role conflict, for supervising data collection and analysis, and for preparing the final manuscript. Susan Gottesmann was instrumental in the development and writing of materials on professionalism and the history of the personnel function. Nelson Olmedillo's major contribution was the interview material dealing with the behavior of personnel managers in conflict situations. James Belasco helped as a general consultant and especially in gathering data on the reliability of the questionnaire.

Special thanks must go to Dean Robert Risley of the New York State School of Industrial and Labor Relations at Cornell University without whose monetary and moral support this study would not have been possible. Equally important to the success of the study was the unstinting support of the American Society for Personnel Administration and its leaders — Bob Berra, Len Brice, and Frank Plasha.

*New Orleans, La.* and *Athens, Ga.*  G.R.
*June 1969*  H.M.T.

# Contents

## CONTENTS

# Introduction

PERSONNEL administration is a practical field and personnel administrators are in the main practical men. Hence, the literature in the field of personnel administration has been dominated by practical utility. This study of the personnel occupations is not in that tradition. The perspective here is theoretical and the goal is to contribute to the theory of personnel administration from the viewpoint of sociology. The findings of this study may be useful to practicing personnel administrators and it is hoped that others, too, will apply the findings to problems in the personnel field. In addition to not being intentionally practical, this research is not focally concerned with personnel administration but rather focuses on the personnel manager. Finally, this is not an exhaustive study of all aspects of the occupation most commonly called personnel manager.

Thus, it is clear what this study is *not* about. What, then, is the purpose of this monograph? It is a study of those aspects of the personnel occupations deemed to be of greatest importance. Essentially, it is concerned with these basic questions:

1. How professional are the personnel occupations? How professional are the individuals who practice personnel administration? (These questions are dealt with in Chapter 3.)

2. How committed are personnel managers to their occupation and their organization? If they are committed in part to both, what are the reasons for this dual commitment? (This topic is the subject of Chapter 4.)

3. How do personnel managers behave in conflict situations? (Chapter 5 deals with data relating to this question from the nation-wide questionnaire; Chapter 6 uses data from in-depth interviews; Chapter 7, dealing with the same question, uses an in-depth analysis of one large company.)

4. What is the occupational image held by personnel managers? Is it an accurate representation of their role? (This query, dealt with throughout the study, is covered in detail in the concluding chapter.)

The data reported in this monograph are based largely on a sixteen-page closed-ended questionnaire survey of the members of the American Society for Personnel Administration (ASPA). (A complete description of the methodology used is given in Appendix A; the questionnaire used is reproduced in Appendix B.) The largest single occupation of ASPA members is the personnel manager and thus much of this study concentrates on it. In Chapter 2 data on vice-presidents of personnel and employment managers are cited primarily as a comparison with data on personnel managers.

Answers to the above basic questions provide much information for personnel managers. Furthermore, they apply to four theoretical aspects of occupational sociology: professionalism, commitment, role conflict resolution, and occupational image.

Throughout the study, there is a dual focus: on personnel management and on occupational sociology. Chapter 1 is an overview of the two fields. In the concluding chapter, contributions to occupational sociology are differentiated from contributions to personnel management. In sum, answers have been sought on a few select sociological questions related to personnel occupations. Hopefully, the findings will make some contribution to both fields.

# AN OCCUPATION IN CONFLICT

*A Study of the Personnel Manager*

# CHAPTER 1

# An Overview
# of the Personnel Occupations
# and Occupational Sociology

THIS study of the personnel occupations in general, with particular attention to a classification most commonly called "personnel manager," has two primary goals:

1. *To contribute, above all, to the field of personnel administration.* Much has been written, but the field has not been the subject of scientific inquiry. This study will make some points about personnel occupations which are contrary to popularly held notions. These are intended to be of value to personnel practitioners, corporate executives, and authors of textbooks on personnel administration.

It is hoped that this study will have the following impacts: (a) personnel administrators will reappraise their roles in their organizations on the basis of these findings; (b) top management will reassess the present role of personnel in the organization; (c) writers of personnel texts will take these findings into consideration in discussing the nature and function of personnel administration.

2. *To contribute to the field of occupational sociology.* Most sociological studies of occupations have been little more than descriptions of their most salient aspects. Although this study includes a certain amount of description, it takes a much broader view. And, in its analysis of the personnel manager, it deals with a series of sociological concepts. For instance, Chapter 3 is concerned with the degree of professionalism among personnel managers. In addition to describing

aspects of their professionalism, it attempts to make some contribution to the theory of professionalism.[1] Similarly, in Chapter 4 the loyalty of personnel managers to both company and occupation is discussed, and in the process Howard Becker's theory of commitment is empirically tested.[2] Chapter 5 looks at the behavior of personnel managers in conflict situations and in so doing makes a contribution to the theory of role conflict resolution developed by Gross, Mason, and McEachern.[3] Finally, in the last chapter, the idea of occupational myth and its existence in the personnel occupations is discussed.[4]

The first section of this chapter gives a brief history of occupational sociology to orient readers in the field of personnel administration; a following section is devoted to a short history of the development of the personnel function; and, finally, there is a summary of the nature and scope of the personnel occupations.

### *History of Occupational Sociology*

A discussion of the ideas of the major intellectual precursors of the field of occupational sociology is important background, even though a hard look into the works of these fathers of sociology reveals little that deals directly with the focal concern of the present study. Marx's interest in worker alienation, Weber's interest in bureaucratic rationality, and Durkheim's concern with the division of labor constitute the major contributions of the sociological giants to occupational sociology.

Marx, Weber, and Durkheim are primarily of historical interest to the field of occupational sociology.[5] More recently it was Robert Park, and Park's influence on Everett Hughes, which gave occupational sociology its major boost. It is Robert Park who, in his book *The City*, led sociology into the study of occupations. The following is an exten-

---

[1]For a good summary of the literature on professionalism, see Howard Vollmer and Donald Mills, *Professionalization* (Englewood Cliffs, N. J.: Prentice-Hall, Inc., 1966).

[2]Howard Becker, "Notes on the Concept of Commitment," *American Journal of Sociology*, vol. 66, 1960, pp. 32–42.

[3]Neal Gross, Ward Mason, and Alexander McEachern, *Explorations in Role Analysis* (New York: John Wiley, Inc., 1958), pp. 244–318.

[4]There are a number of articles which deal with occupational myth. See, for example, Richard Simpson and Ida Simpson, "The Psychiatric Attendant: Development of an Occupational Self Image in a Low State Occupation," *American Sociological Review*, vol. 24, 1959, pp. 389–393.

[5]Other theorists of historical interest to occupational sociology are G. Simmel and T. Veblen. An extensive history of occupational sociology should include their influence as well as the impact of a number of other sociological theorists.

sive quotation from *The City* which is cited in its entirety because it is one of the bases of occupational sociology:

> Every device which facilitates trade and industry prepares the way for a further division of labor and so tends further to specialize the tasks in which men find their vocations.
>
> The outcome of this process is to break down or modify the older social and economic organization of society, which was based on family ties, local associations, on culture, caste, and status, and to substitute for it an organization based on occupation and vocational interests.
>
> In the city every vocation, even that of a beggar, tends to assume the character of a profession and the discipline which success in any vocation imposes, together with the associations that it enforces, emphasizes this tendency — the tendency, namely, not merely to specialize, but to rationalize one's occupation and to develop a specific and conscious technique for carrying it on.
>
> The effect of the vocations and the division of labor is to produce, in the first instance, not social groups, but vocational types: the actor, the plumber, and the lumber-jack. The organizations like the trade and the labor unions which men of the same trade or profession form, are based on common interests. In this respect they differ from forms of association like the neighborhood, which are based on contiguity, personal association, and the common ties of humanity. The different trades and professions seem disposed to group themselves in classes, that is to say, the artisan, business, and professional classes. But in the modern democratic state the classes have as yet attained no effective organization. Socialism, founded on an effort to create an organization based on "class consciousness," has never succeeded, except, perhaps in Russia, in creating more than a political party.
>
> The effects of the division of labor as a discipline, i.e., as means of molding character, may therefore be best studied in the vocational types it has produced. Among the types which it would be interesting to study are: the shopgirl, the policeman, the peddler, the cab-man, the night-watchman, the clairvoyant, the vaudeville performer, the labor agitator, the quack doctor, the bartender, the ward boss, the strike-breaker, the school teacher, the reporter, the stockbroker, the pawnbroker; all of these are characteristic poducts of the conditions of city life; each, with its special experience, insight, and point of view determines for each vocational group and for the city as a whole its individuality.[6]

[6]Robert Park, Ernest Burgess, and Roderick McKenzie, *The City* (Chicago: University of Chicago Press, 1925), pp. 13–14.

*3*

Park's orientation led to a number of studies of occupations, of which the most famous are of the hobo,[7] the taxi-dance hall girl,[8] and the professional thief.[9] In Peter Berger's view, a critical turning point is Cottrell's study of the railroader which marked the transition from the study of disreputable to reputable occupations. It is from this point on, according to Berger, that occupational sociology moves out of the exclusive domain of the University of Chicago.[10]

Under the influence of Park and the Chicago School of Sociology, Everett Hughes emerged as the major force in occupational sociology. In an article in the *American Journal of Sociology* in 1928, Hughes discussed the following topics which became focal concerns of occupational sociology: (a) occupational culture, (b) colleagueship, (c) occupational selection, (d) the secularized division of labor of contemporary society, (e) backgrounds of individuals entering specific occupations, (f) mobility, (g) a typology of different levels of our division of labor, (h) occupation and personality, (i) professionalization, (j) career patterns.[11]

In a later article in the same journal, Hughes gave a rather concise statement of his interest in occupations in general and career patterns in particular:

> a study of careers — of the moving perspective in which persons orient themselves with reference to the social order, and of the typical sequences and concatenations of office — may be expected to reveal the nature and "working constitution" of a society. Institutions are but the forms in which the collective behavior and collective action of people go on. In the course of a career the person finds his place within these forms, carries on his active life with reference to other people, and interprets the meaning of the one life he has to live.[12]

Everett Hughes has continued to be interested in occupational sociology and remains productive. Above all, he has interested a number of his students in occupational sociology. Due in great part to his

[7]Nels Aronson, *The Hobo* (Chicago: University of Chicago Press, 1923).

[8]Paul Cressy, *The Taxi-Dance Hall* (Chicago: University of Chicago Press, 1932).

[9]Edwin Sutherland, *The Professional Thief* (Chicago: University of Chicago Press, 1937).

[10]Peter Berger, *The Human Shape of Work* (New York: Macmillan Co., 1964), p. 226.

[11]Reprinted in Everett Hughes, *Men and Their Work* (Glencoe, Ill.: Free Press, 1958), pp. 23–41.

[12]*ibid.*, p. 67.

urging, there has been a proliferation of studies of particular occupations.

A recent article has compared the status of occupational sociology between 1946–1952 and 1953–1959 on the basis of writings in the field.[13] The two time periods are compared in terms of published articles on occupational groups:

|  | 1946–1952 | 1953–1959 |
|---|---|---|
| Professional persons | 58% | 48% |
| Proprietors, managers, and officials | 18 | 22 |
| Clerks and kindred workers | 3 | 2 |
| Skilled workers and foremen | 3 | 2 |
| Semiskilled | 8 | 7 |
| Unskilled | 1 | 10 |
| Military | 9 | 9 |

Clearly, the major changes have been the decline in concentration on professions and the increased interest in unskilled workers.

The following comparison of the writings in the two time periods is given in terms of subject matter:

|  | 1946–1952 | 1953–1959 |
|---|---|---|
| Career | 23% | 13% |
| Status and mobility | 14 | 21 |
| Ethnic | 13 | 8 |
| Working force | 11 | 8 |
| Occupational role and personality | 9 | 16 |
| Occupation comparisons | 4 | 5 |
| Methodology | 4 | 8 |
| Client-professional relations | 3 | 1 |
| Occupation culture and ethics | 2 | 10 |
| Miscellaneous | 10 | 5 |

Thus the growing fields in occupational sociology appear to be: status and mobility, occupational role and personality, methodology, occupational culture and ethics. Declining in interest are such topics as career and, most surprisingly, ethnic occupational issues.

There is increased theoretical orientation in the period 1953–1959. In 1946–1952 a fourth of the articles lacked a theoretical orientation. In contrast, in the more recent period, less than a twentieth of the articles lacked a theoretical framework. The social structural orientation grew in popularity from 13 to 31 percent in 1953–1959. Role

[13]Erwin Smigel, *et al.*, "Occupational Sociology: A Reexamination," *Sociology and Social Research*, vol. 47, July 1963, pp. 472–477.

theory has grown comparably from 7 to 21 percent. In contrast, the historical approach has diminished in use from 10 to 4 percent. Finally, there is a greater use of statistics in the later period. The present study is clearly in the main stream since it deals with role theory and extensively uses statistical techniques.

## History of Personnel

The function of providing manpower resources and effective leadership in their utilization, in the interest of developing a highly motivated and smooth-running work force, is performed by all supervisors, managers, and executives of an organization, but is institutionalized in a personnel department. In organizations that are large enough to warrant it, personnel practitioners are employed in a separate staff unit or department. Therefore, the growth of the personnel occupation parallels, in general, the development and growth of the modern organization and, specifically, the development and growth of the personnel department and its function within organizations. In examining the historical development of personnel, as a separate occupation within an organization, an attempt will be made to: describe the factors contributing to the growth of the personnel department; describe the increase in the body of knowledge regarding human behavior that affects personnel policies and procedures; show how the trends that affect the development of the personnel function led, also, to the development of numerous specializations within the personnel field.

The beginnings of personnel, and the problems that led to its creation, did not arise until large aggregations of people came to work together in one organization. The spread of large-scale organizations in the American economy dates from the beginning of the twentieth century. This, then, is a convenient starting point for the history of personnel. Prior to and during World War I, two factors contributed to the rise of the employment management department, the predecessor of the modern personnel department. They were found by both Eilbirt,[14] and F. B. Miller and M. A. Coghill[15] to be "welfarism" and "scientific management."

[14]Henry Eilbirt, "The Development of Personnel Management in the United States," *Business History Review*, vol. 33, no. 3 (Autumn 1959), pp. 345–364.

[15]Frank B. Miller and Mary Ann Coghill, "Sex and the Personnel Manager," *Industrial and Labor Relations Review*, vol. 18, no. 1 (October 1964), and Frank B. Miller and Mary Ann Coghill, *The Historical Sources of Personnel Work*, (Ithaca, N. Y.: New York State School of Industrial and Labor Relations, Cornell University, September 1961).

Welfarism, or paternalism, a movement found both in society at large and within industries, was

> aimed at improving the general tenor of American living and the standards of the poor and unfortunate.... In essence, welfare work sought to ameliorate the hardworking life... Towards this end, management made available various facilities such as libraries and other recreational premises, offered financial assistance for education... provided medical care and instituted hygienic measures.[16]

Also, during this period most of the states passed workmen's compensation laws which

> hold the employer financially responsible for all injuries occurring to workers while on the job.... The passage of these laws was a prime force in causing employers to take positive steps to reduce and prevent work injuries and to organize company health programs. Thus the creation of such positions as safety engineer, safety director, company physician, industrial nurse, and medical director.[17]

To institute and supervise such measures, and to serve as a personal contact between the increasingly large numbers of employees and employers, became the responsibility of social or welfare secretaries. These separate staff middlemen positions were filled by persons with philanthropic and social work backgrounds. They were the forerunners of the modern personnel administrator.

Alongside this new view of increasing the lot of the worker came industry's desire to increase its efficiency and profit through improved methods of managing employees. The scientific management school, led by Frederick W. Taylor, claimed that hidden wastes in an organization, and resultant costs, were caused by the inefficient use of labor. By using time and motion studies, instead of relying on personal judgments of operating linesmen, work could be systematically and objectively analyzed. These studies helped to provide a basis, also, for more efficient training and supervising.

The central tenet of Taylor's theory was man's profit motive. He reasoned that the more closely pay was related to work effort and output, the harder a man would work and the more he would produce.

> Various methods of measuring worker output and ways of relating pay to it were devised....(1) pay should be on merit of per-

[16]Henry Eilbirt, "The Development of Personnel Management in the United States," *Management of the Personnel Function*, I. L. Heckmann and S. G. Hunery- ager, eds. (Columbus, Ohio: Charles E. Merrill Books, 1962), p. 11.

[17]Dale S. Beach, *Personnel: The Management of People at Work* (New York: Macmillan Co., 1965), p. 24.

formance....(2) the time unit should be as small as possible....The ideal situation is piece-work wages in which pay is directly dependent on the actual amount of work accomplished.[18]

## Employment management

The shift of attention from welfare management to scientific management resulted about 1912 in the development of employment management departments.[19] Such departments grew in number and in functions assigned to them during this period and up to about 1925. The core functions of these departments were recruiting, selection, job placement, and record keeping. Some companies also relegated to them the administration of the welfare program, the training program, and the settlement of complaints and grievances. These functions grew out of: (a) Taylor's demand for proper selection and placement of workers on jobs where they could be superior producers; (b) the demands created by World War I for thousands of workers; (c) the high cost of labor turnover; (d) the need to relieve overworked foremen of the tasks of hiring and firing. These multiple-function departments became the forerunners of the modern personnel departments.

Following World War I, two other major developments arose simultaneously which still have a bearing on the personnel field — the use of psychological tests for selection and the so-called "American plan" of welfare capitalism.

## Industrial psychology

The field of industrial psychology, receiving its impetus in 1913 from the publication of Hugo Munsterberg's *Psychology and Industrial Efficiency*,[20] created tests to measure suitability of applicants for specific job vacancies. The principles of industrial psychology applied to employment, job placement, and promotion, and also to training. The use of industrial psychology was accelerated during World War I by the need both to place draftees on jobs to which they were best suited, and to train them quickly and efficiently to handle those jobs. This technically augmented function was assigned to personnel departments.

[18]Amitai Etzioni, *Modern Organizations* (Englewood Cliffs, N. J.: Prentice-Hall, 1964), p. 22.

[19]Ordway Tead, "Personnel Administration," *Encyclopedia of the Social Sciences*, vol. 12, New York, 1934, p. 88.

[20]Houghton Mifflin, Boston and New York, 1913.

## The American plan

The American plan was developed by large companies in the 1920's to offset the growing power of trade unions. It established employee representation plans (ERP-company unions) to "provide a type of grievance procedure and to give employees a voice in decisions affecting the work force"[21] and it included increased employee welfare measures. Although the motives were perhaps less noble than those of welfarism, the effect on the worker was the same. Personnel departments became the administrators of the American plan. By the end of the 1920's, the personnel function, as it had come to be called, was firmly established.

## Unionism

With the 1930's came the Great Depression, increased union organization, the formation of the CIO, and the Wagner Act of 1935. The Wagner Act gave public policy endorsement to collective bargaining and to elections, under National Labor Relations Board mandate, to settle the issue of union representation in companies where more than one union competed for the right to represent the employees. In the late 1930's and 1940's, in response to these events, new departments of labor relations were created either as adjuncts to personnel departments under the same administrative head, or as divisions within personnel departments.

## Government legislation

During the 1930's and 1940's, increased federal legislation forced changes in the benefits and training functions of personnel departments, as well as a new rationale for wage and salary administration.

The field of benefits, already created by welfarism and the American plan, increased in scope with the passage of the Social Security Act of 1936. With World War II, the Training Within Industry (TWI) program was developed. It "provided training course outlines and materials covering subjects such as job relations (human relations), job instruction, and job methods (work simplification)."[22]

The Fair Labor Standards Act of 1938, in part a response to trends in union demands in collective bargaining and in grievances, provided minimum wage rates and overtime compensation. It forced manage-

[21]George Strauss and Leonard Sayles, *Personnel: The Human Problem of Management* (Englewood Cliffs, N. J.: Prentice-Hall, 1967), p. 426.

[22]Herbert J. Chruden and Arthur W. Sherman, Jr., *Personnel Management* (Cincinnati: South-Western Publishing Co., 1959), p. 11.

ment to adopt well organized, defensible compensation programs. And World War II forced wages to be placed under the War Labor Board. In the course of resolving disputes and later administering the wage stabilization program,

> the War Labor Board formulated a number of sound principles that were used in arriving at wage decisions....In many cases the board directed that companies establish formal wage structures, job evaluation programs, and reasonable pay administration policies.[23]

The result of these trends of unionism and government legislation was to increase, in number and scope, the functions assigned to personnel departments.

*Human Relations school*

Recent trends in personnel, since 1950, are outgrowths of the Human Relations school and the increased role and influence of the behavioral sciences in industry. Included in these trends are: increased research capacity and interest; management development; public and community relations; manpower and organizational planning. This emphasis on the ideas prevalent in the behavioral sciences grew out of a reaction to the classical and formal approach (e.g. scientific management).

Elton Mayo, the father of the school, and his associates discovered that (a) the amount of work carried out by a worker (hence, his level of efficiency) is not determined solely by his physical capacity, but also by his social capacity; (b) noneconomic rewards play a central role in determining the motivation and the happiness of the worker; (c) the highest specialization is by no means the most efficient form of the division of labor; (d) workers do not react to management and its norms and rewards as individuals, but as members of groups. Above all, the Human Relations school emphasized the roles of communication, participation, and leadership in encouraging employee productivity.[24]

These conclusions were the result of many field and experimental studies conducted by social scientists. The most famous of these is Roethlisberger and Dickson's study of Western Electric's Hawthorne works, published in 1939 as *Management and the Worker*.[25] Its effect on the functions assigned to the personnel department has been two-

---

[23]Beach, p. 30.

[24]*ibid.*

[25]F. J. Roethlisberger and W. J. Dickson, *Management and the Worker* (Cambridge, Mass.: Harvard University Press, 1939).

*10*

fold. First, it forced the creation of both an internal (company publications) and external (community and public relations) communications function. Second, a personnel research department was created to go more deeply into such topics as human motivation, leadership, job satisfaction, group relations, communication, supervision, and discipline. The systematic body of knowledge in the field of human relations has been developing and growing. As the behavioral sciences (sociology, psychology, social psychology) are applied to the study of industrial man, the field has come to be retitled "organizational behavior."

The early history of the growth of the personnel occupations can be summarized in three general prevailing trends: the "welfare trend" which emphasized personnel as the department for helping people in an organization and was further strengthened by government legislation; the "trash-can trend" which dumped burdensome or unpleasant tasks, not clearly assigned to any other department, into personnel; and the "professionalization trend" which grew out of the demand for expertise in union negotiations, application of industrial psychology and other behavioral sciences, and recent management recognition of the essential part personnel plays in carrying out provisions of new federal and state legislation (i.e. Equal Opportunity Employment Act and Manpower Training and Development Act). The diversified image and mission of the personnel department today reflects these historical trends.

### Nature and Scope of Personnel

When specialized departments were created in the 1920's and 1930's to handle the administration of personnel programs, they were usually called personnel departments, rather than employment management. With the addition of the labor relations function to the other activities of the personnel department, the designation was often changed to industrial relations department. Today, in companies where either no union exists or where labor relations is a separate staff function, the department may still be called the personnel department.[26] In this study, personnel and industrial relations are used interchangeably.

From the historical review in the preceding section, it can be seen that in the development of the personnel occupation many specialties accrued to this field. The scope of these assignments is shown in the following descriptions of the major specialties in personnel.

[26]Beach, p. 54.

*Employment and placement*

This area includes recruitment, selection, placement, orientation, personnel ratings, job analysis, job description, transfers, and termination. Its purpose is "to control the flow of people in and out of the various jobs in the organization."[27] It has a direct effect on the quality and quantity of the people in the organization. Very often it is broken down into two divisions that control the management (salaried) level and the nonmanagement (hourly) level.

*Training and development*

"Training in organizations is the process of applying the appropriate educational method to those situations in an organization in which improved performance (production) can result from better learning."[28] This specialty includes among its duties: induction, on-the-job training, supervisory training, and management development.

*Wage and salary administration*

The purpose of this specialty is to compensate employees for their services, in an attempt to direct and motivate them to attain desired standards of performance and behavior.[29] The derivative duties of wage and salary include: installing and designing job evaluation programs, and periodic wage and salary surveys both internally and externally in companies in similar industries or in the same geographical area.

*Benefits and services*

Most firms are required by labor contracts and/or various laws to provide fringe benefits to their employees. Benefits and services is primarily responsible for administering insurance, health, hospitalization, medical care, pension, and retirement plans.

*Personnel research*

The central focus of personnel research is to conduct studies of personnel policies, programs, and practices and to examine how these

[27]From Professor James Belasco, personal communication, "Personnel Administration: An Interview," Course GMP–1602, Graduate School of Business, University of Buffalo, May 15, 1968.

[28]Professor Emil Mesic's definition as given in his course ILR 423, Fall 1966, Design and Administration of Training Programs, Cornell University.

[29]D. W. Belcher, *Wage and Salary Administration* (Englewood Cliffs, N. J.: Prentice-Hall, 1955), pp. 15–24.

can be made to contribute more effectively to the goals of the organization.

### Safety

Within any organization, the employer has a responsibility to maintain the kind of physical establishment that provides the best working conditions from a safety point of view. The safety specialty, therefore, coordinates accident prevention programs, checks for conditions hazardous to employees, and conducts a safety education program for both supervisors and employees.

### Labor relations

This specialty is concerned primarily with negotiating formal written agreements and contracts with the unions, and for the daily administration of these agreements. Such contracts usually fix the price of labor, hours and working conditions, and introduce employee initiative into the relationship between employees and employers.

### Basic Functions of Personnel

### Staff function

The personnel department, as a staff function, operates to help the line or operating departments perform their jobs more effectively. As such, its authority is theoretically confined to advising, counseling, and assistance. The supervisors need not abide by the recommendations or advice given by the personnel department. "Nevertheless, like any staff official, the personnel man's authority for specialized help soon becomes accepted if for no other reason than he is a specialist in one particular area."[30] Thus, the scope of the effectiveness of his advice is bounded by his recognized competency.

### Control function

Two control activities given to personnel, and identified by Strauss and Sayles in their book, *Personnel*, are the audit and stabilization functions.[31] In its auditing activity, it appraises how well managers have been doing their jobs, *after the fact*. In performing its stabilization function, personnel makes sure all policies are being administered properly, by giving permission "to go ahead" only *after* personnel has

---

[30]I. L. Heckmann and S. G. Huneryager, *Management of the Personnel Function* (Columbus, Ohio: Charles E. Merrill Books, 1962), p. 6.
[31]Strauss and Sayles, p. 435.

*13*

seen and passed on all requests from other departments to act on personnel matters.

*Service or functional authority*

In addition to its staff and control activities, personnel has been granted functional authority for particular services or activities. It is these service functions, such as planning company picnics, record keeping, and handling the cafeteria, that Dalton McFarland refers to as the "trash-can" functions which are, in his words, "a broad array of functions having little to do with the major goals of personnel administration."[32]

*Policy initiation and formulation*

The executive in charge of the personnel function, be he the vice-president in charge of personnel at the corporate level or a personnel manager at either a local plant level or in a small company, is usually in charge of policy initiation and formulation. He proposes and drafts new policies or revisions to cover recurring problems or to prevent anticipated new ones. But it is usually only through a top line official that the policy is issued and instituted.

[32]Dalton McFarland, *Conflict and Cooperation in Personnel Administration* (New York: American Foundation for Management Research, 1962), p. 49.

# CHAPTER 2

# Some General Findings

THE data reported in this study are based primarily on responses from personnel administrators who are members of the American Society for Personnel Administration. Major emphasis was placed on obtaining a high response rate among personnel managers since this is the dominant group in ASPA. The only other sizable groups within ASPA are vice-presidents of personnel and employment managers, neither of which received the additional follow-up stimuli given personnel managers. (See Appendix A for a discussion of the follow-up techniques used.) Consequently, the response rates for these two groups are lower than for the personnel managers. Since the function of these data is to highlight and put into perspective the findings on personnel managers, it is freely admitted that data on the two subgroups are less complete.

A vice-president of personnel is generally the top corporate official of the personnel department. A personnel manager is, in general, the top personnel official at a particular location. In many cases a personnel manager may supervise personnel matters at his location and report to a vice-president of personnel. An employment manager is a specialist in charge of recruiting and hiring personnel. In general, an employment manager is subordinate to the personnel manager and reports directly to him.

Of the 93 vice-presidents of personnel in ASPA, 51 responded to the questionnaire (a response rate of 55 percent). Of 132 employment managers, 60 returned completed questionnaires (response rate of 45 percent). Although these response rates do not rival the return from personnel managers (66 percent or 419 of 623 sampled), they are useful as a basis for comparison.

The following is a breakdown of the three groups, by age spans:

| Age | Personnel Manager | Employment Manager | Vice-President |
|---|---|---|---|
| 20–29 ....... | 5% | 13% | 4% |
| 30–49 ....... | 71% | 69% | 55% |
| 50–69 ....... | 24% | 18% | 41% |

Most personnel managers and employment managers are between the ages of thirty and forty-nine. A comparatively larger proportion of vice-presidents are over fifty. The slightly larger percentage of employment managers in the twenty to twenty-nine age group suggests that this is sometimes an entry job. It is not clear from this classification if there is a pattern of career progression.

Among the three classifications, the employment manager has been in his occupation the fewest number of years. Employment managers were on their present jobs an average of 2.8 years, while both vice-presidents and personnel managers were on theirs an average of 5 years. This finding would seem to reflect the "stepping-stone" nature of the employment manager position, in general, it is not the ultimate career goal. On the other hand, both the personnel manager and vice-president positions may be viewed as terminal.

The following are comparisons of their educational levels:

| Highest Educational Level Achieved | Personnel Manager | Employment Manager | Vice-President |
|---|---|---|---|
| High school graduate ....... | 4% | — | 4% |
| Some college—college graduate | 47% | 47% | 32% |
| Some advanced work— advanced degree .......... | 49% | 53% | 64% |

The only significant difference among the three groups is the greater likelihood of vice-presidents of personnel to have postgraduate education (consequently, fewer were merely college graduates). This may simply be a by-product of their greater age. About 60 percent in each group majored in personnel administration or the related fields of behavioral science or business administration while in college.

An examination of the educational level of the respondents' fathers results in the following:

| Father's Education | Personnel Manager | Employment Manager | Vice-President |
|---|---|---|---|
| Less than grade school ...... | 21% | 23% | 25% |
| Grade school ............... | 29% | 43% | 27% |
| Some high school .......... | 21% | 8% | 18% |
| Some college—college graduate | 23% | 23% | 26% |
| Some advanced work— advanced degree .......... | 6% | 3% | 4% |

Of major interest is the high proportion of fathers of employment managers who have no more than a grade school education. This may indicate that employment managers often come from different social backgrounds than personnel managers or vice-presidents of personnel. The educational levels of the fathers of personnel managers and vice-presidents are very similar.

It is pertinent, also, to examine the occupations of the respondents' fathers:

| Father's Occupation | Personnel Manager | Employment Manager | Vice-President |
|---|---|---|---|
| Professional—semiprofessional | 20% | 17% | 45% |
| Managers, officials, proprietors | 34% | 23% | 25% |
| Clerical—sales | 8% | 7% | 26% |
| Craftsmen—foremen, operatives, household, service, laborers, etc. | 38% | 53% | 4% |

Here is potent evidence that the three groups come from different social backgrounds. Vice-presidents are much more likely to have fathers in professional or semiprofessional occupations. Personnel managers are more likely to have fathers who are managers, officials, or proprietors. The blue-collar category of occupations was more likely for the fathers of employment managers. Strikingly few of the vice-presidents' fathers were blue-collar workers. Now it is possible to assume that there is not a continuous career progression from employment manager to vice-president. Rather it would appear that only individuals with certain background characteristics are likely to become vice-presidents. Evidence on this point is not conclusive in this study, but certainly suggestive.

The salary distributions for the three groups were as follows:

| Salary | Personnel Manager | Employment Manager | Vice-President |
|---|---|---|---|
| Under $10,000 | 10% | 20% | 15% |
| $10,000–19,999 | 76% | 67% | 40% |
| $20,000–24,999 | 10% | 9% | 45% |
| $25,000 and up | 4% | 4% | — |

A surprising number of vice-presidents earn less than $10,000 a year. It is also remarkable that none of the vice-presidents earns more than $25,000, while 4 percent of both personnel managers and employment managers earn more than that figure. The majority of both personnel managers and employment managers earn between $10,000 and $20,000. Significantly more vice-presidents earn between $20,000 and $25,000.

The question has already been raised of whether there is, in fact, a career pattern continuum from employment manager to vice-president of personnel. The following chart, which details the percentage in each group who had experience in each of the major subfields of personnel, sheds some light on this question:

| Past Experience in Subfields of Personnel | Personnel Manager | Employment Manager | Vice-President |
|---|---|---|---|
| Vice-president of personnel level ................... | 0% | 3% | — |
| Personnel management level ................... | — | 25% | 92% |
| Employment management level ................... | 27% | — | 24% |
| Wage and salary ............ | 12% | 18% | 10% |
| Training ................. | 8% | 10% | 12% |
| Labor relations ............. | 12% | 5% | 14% |
| Benefits ................... | 4% | 5% | 0% |
| Other .................... | 6% | 5% | 6% |

In general, it may be concluded that *no* clear career pattern emerges. The strongest tendency is for vice-presidents of personnel to have been personnel managers at some time in their careers. There is some tendency for both personnel managers and vice-presidents to have spent time in employment. Surprisingly, 25 percent of employment managers were personnel managers at one time. Two possible explanations of this phenomenon are that a personnel manager in a small company might accept an employment management position in a large company or, less likely, that those employment managers were personnel managers who had been demoted.

The majority of respondents in each of the three groups came from companies primarily engaged in manufacturing. A much higher percentage of vice-presidents are found in either finance or insurance. This difference may be attributable to a tendency of such organizations to use more freely the title of vice-president.

A look at the distribution of the three groups by size of company, based on number of employees, shows:

| Number of Employees in Company | Personnel Manager | Employment Manager | Vice-President |
|---|---|---|---|
| Under 1,000 ................ | 43% | 22% | 22% |
| 1,000–4,999 ............... | 36% | 41% | 54% |
| 5,000 plus ................ | 21% | 37% | 24% |

Personnel managers are likely to be in small companies. This may be because small companies may have only one personnel man who performs all personnel functions with or without a secretary and is called personnel manager. In contrast, the employment manager is more a position of larger organizations. The larger organizations may be more likely to afford an employment specialist.

The preceding discussion has described the differences, as well as the similarities, among the three occupations. The following data give a more detailed view of the personnel manager.

Personnel managers were asked to distribute their working hours per week among typical personnel activities. The following are the percentages of time they actually spend on each, feel they should spend on each, and the differences:

| Activity | Actual % | Should % | Difference |
|---|---|---|---|
| Supervising subordinates ............... | 17% | 14% | −3% |
| Planning personnel department activities | 16% | 20% | +4% |
| Representing company to outside organizations ....................... | 5% | 6% | +1% |
| Representing company to the union ..... | 10% | 9% | −1% |
| Gathering information both inside and outside the organization ............. | 10% | 6% | −4% |
| Providing information and advice for decision-making by others ........... | 17% | 19% | +2% |
| Making decisions on personnel matters for other departments in the company | 13% | 11% | −2% |
| Involved in professional functions ....... | 4% | 5% | +1% |
| Others ............................... | 8% | 10% | +2% |

One interesting figure is the high percentage of time actually spent on making decisions for others (13 percent). This relatively high figure is remarkable considering the contention of many personnel managers that they make recommendations, not decisions. It will have a bearing upon the later discussion of behavior in conflict situations. The most striking finding, however, in the above percentages is the lack of differences. Apparently personnel managers are, in the main, satisfied with the time they spend on personnel activities. Despite their satisfaction some of the differences are interesting. Looking at activities in which personnel managers feel they should be working harder, the biggest difference appears to be in "planning personnel department activities." This seems to reflect their desire to work on longer range and broader questions relating to the personnel function and a desire to "represent the company to outside organizations." These data seem to indicate an aspiration to loftier status in the organization.

More time to be spent in "providing information and advice for decision-making by others" seems to reaffirm the personnel manager's *raison d'être*. It is the most typical and traditional function of personnel work, the one stressed by most texts, teachers, and practitioners. This emphasis is at variance with other findings in this study, as will be shown later.

The wish for more "involvement in professional personnel functions" reflects a trend in the field toward professionalism. This is discussed at some length in the next chapter.

The areas in which personnel managers feel they should be spending less time are interrelated. "Supervising subordinates," "gathering information," "representing the company to the union" apparently represent to our respondents trivial and/or unpopular demands. The decline in "making decisions for others" is related to the increase in "providing information for decision-making by others." These all mirror the time-hallowed occupational image of personnel managers — that they should be advisors and not decision-makers. The high percentage of time spent on decision-making belies this image. Nevertheless, when questioned, personnel managers tend to adhere to the image and claim they wish to do less decision-making.

Similar data were gathered on the personnel manager's view of how other persons in the organization influence his activities. The respondents were presented with five members of the organization and asked to rate them, from one to five, in terms of their influence on the respondent's activities. The following are the mean rankings (the lower the ranking, the greater the influence):

| | |
|---|---|
| Your immediate supervisor | 1.7 |
| Yourself | 1.9 |
| Other management officials | 3.2 |
| Your subordinate(s) | 3.9 |
| Other personnel people | 4.0 |

Several observations should be made about these findings. (1) It is interesting that the respondent himself is not the major influence on his activities. This has implications on his degree of professionalism since one characteristic of the professional is autonomy. Looking at the established professions, it is difficult to imagine a doctor, for instance, ranking anyone but himself as the major determiner of his activities. (2) The fact that the supervisor is ranked first clearly reaffirms the primarily bureaucratic nature of the occupation. Bureaucratic occupations face important barriers to professionalism. (3) The low ranking of the other personnel positions again indicates the nonprofessionalism of personnel managers. In a profession, others in the occupation have a major influence.

The respondents were also asked how much influence each of the significant others *should* have on their activities. The following is a summary of the means for the *actual*, the *should*, and the *differences* (the range again is one to five, with a lower mean score indicating greater influence):

|  | Actual | Should | Differences |
|---|---|---|---|
| Yourself | 1.9 | 1.8 | –.1 |
| Your subordinate(s) | 3.9 | 3.8 | –.1 |
| Other personnel people | 4.0 | 4.0 | — |
| Your immediate supervisor | 1.7 | 1.9 | –.2 |
| Other management officials | 3.2 | 3.4 | –.2 |

The *difference* scores seem to offer some hope for professionalism. Personnel managers feel that their superior and other management officials should have less influence and, on the other hand, that the self and subordinates should have more. All of these choices tend toward professionalism, the subject of the next chapter.

Here, by way of highlights, is a summary chart of cross-occupational comparisons covered in this chapter.

|  | Personnel Manager | Employment Manager | Vice-Presidents |
|---|---|---|---|
| Number responding | 419 | 60 | 51 |
| Percentage responding | 66% | 45% | 55% |
| Age (% between 20–29) | 5% | 13% | 4% |
| Age (% between 30–49) | 71% | 69% | 55% |
| Age (% between 50–69) | 24% | 18% | 41% |
| Education (% some college—college graduate) | 47% | 47% | 32% |
| Education (% some advanced work—advanced degree) | 49% | 53% | 64% |
| College major (% in personnel or related fields) | 65% | 64% | 58% |
| Father's education (% grade school—or less) | 50% | 66% | 52% |
| Father's occupation (% professional—semiprofessional) | 20% | 17% | 45% |

|  | Personnel Manager | Employment Manager | Vice-Presidents |
|---|---|---|---|
| Father's occupation (% craftsmen, foremen, operatives, household, service, laborers, etc.) | 38% | 53% | 4% |
| Salary (% $10,000–19,999) | 76% | 67% | 41% |
| Salary (% $20,000 and up) | 14% | 13% | 45% |
| Percent having experience as a personnel manager | — | 25% | 92% |
| Percent having experience as an employment manager | 27% | — | 24% |
| Size of company (% in companies with 0–999 employees) | 43% | 22% | 22% |
| Size of company (% in companies with more than 5,000 employees) | 21% | 37% | 24% |

# CHAPTER 3

# Professionalism in the Personnel Occupations

PROFESSIONALISM is discussed here at two levels: the *occupational* and the *individual*. At the *occupational* level there are a number of evolutionary stages toward full professionalism. How far the personnel occupations have progressed in this process will be examined.

In every occupation, *individuals* vary in their degree of professionalism. Thus, in the highly professional occupation of medicine, it is possible to have nonprofessional doctors. Conversely, in the nonprofessional janitorial occupation, one might find a highly professional janitor. The second focus will be on the degree of professionalism of individual personnel managers.

## Measurement of Occupational Professionalism

To evaluate the degree of professionalism of the personnel *occupation*, two analytical tools may be employed: one historical and the other ahistorical. One theoretical approach from each method will be used.

The historical approach formulated by Wilensky measures the degree of professionalism by how consistently an occupation follows a given sequence of events in its development.[1] The first stage of the Wilensky process is the *creation of a full-time occupation*. According to Tead, this occurred in personnel in 1912, with the creation of the first employment management department.[2] Practitioners of this occu-

[1]Harold Wilensky, "The Professionalization of Everyone?" *AJS*, vol. 70, no. 2 (September 1964), p. 145.

[2]Ordway Tead, "Personnel Administration," *Encyclopedia of the Social Sciences*, vol. 12, New York, 1934, p. 88.

pation were originally social or welfare secretaries; thus, as Wilensky suggests, the new practitioners were amateurs previously employed in other tasks. The employment management department, Tead further suggests, arose from the needs of society (welfarism) and of organization (scientific management). This development closely approximates the first stage of Wilensky's schema.

The second stage is the *establishment of a training school.* Here, personnel followed the lead of the established professions because the main impetus came from the first local personnel association, the Boston Employment Managers' Association, which

> prevailed on several eastern universities to develop programs in employment management. The first institution to respond was the Amos Tuck School at Dartmouth College.[3]

This pioneering program was first introduced in the autumn of 1915.[3] As in other university affiliated schools, certain core academic programs were established,[4] academic degrees awarded, and university bureaus devoted to personnel research established.[5] A corps of teachers developed to train people in proper employment methods, rather than to do research.[6] The first of these were leaders in a movement to train people in employment techniques initiated by the federal government, which arose from the World War I need to hire and train workers in large numbers for shipyards and munitions works recently taken over by the government.

From this beginning in 1915 and through the Second World War, the emphasis on techniques and procedures formed the crux of personnel education.[7] There was, however, during this time latent interest in an approach that stressed general theory and fundamental concepts, rather than a how-to-do-it approach:

> But this more general approach to personnel education at the conceptual level had, necessarily, to await advances in research, theory

[3]Cyril Curtis Ling, *The Management of Personnel Relations—History and Origins* (Homewood, Ill.: Richard Irwin, Inc., 1965), p. 377.

[4]For a description of the thirteen "typical" or "most popular" course categories, see Kenneth E. Schnelle and Harland Fox, "University Courses in Industrial Relations," *Personnel Journal,* vol. 30, September 1951, p. 129.

[5]For further explanation of this, see Ling, pp. 396–400.

[6]As witnessed by a report of a "Conference of Personnel Teachers" as reported by Ordway Tead, "The Problems of Graduate Training in Personnel Administration," *Journal of Political Economy,* vol. 29, May 1921, p. 359.

[7]Ling, p. 392.

and teaching of the behavioral sciences...these advances did not really get underway until the implications of the Hawthorne experiments began to be understood and until greater maturity in labor relations started to appear during the 1940's.[8]

Thus, although the structure of a university training school appeared early, as it did in the established professions, a systematic body of theory was absent until the later stages of its development.

After the establishment of the first local personnel association in Boston in 1912, a dozen other cities established local associations. Leaders from these several groups met in 1918 to form the *first national personnel association,* the third stage in Wilensky's schema. This group called itself the National Association of Employment Managers. Later it changed its name to the Industrial Relations Association of America. Then it disbanded, but managed to revive and change its name to the National Personnel Association. Once again, in 1923, it was restructured and renamed the American Management Association. From 1923 to 1948, personnel had no national organization of its own, except the personnel division of the American Management Association.

In 1948, however, the American Society for Personnel Administration (ASPA) was formed by a group of ninety-two persons engaged in the field of personnel and industrial relations. Its first conference was held in June 1949 in Cleveland, Ohio. Although incorporated in Ohio, the national offices were not located in Berea, Ohio until January of 1965. Previously, they were in Milwaukee and East Lansing, Michigan. The Society grew from approximately 3,000 members in 1964 to its present membership of approximately 4,500, an increase of 50 percent in four years. It is the only national organization of personnel and industrial relations executives in private industry. It has members in all fifty states and in fifteen foreign countries. The Society's stated purposes are: to strive for higher standards of performance; to provide a central, national, clearing house of authoritative data and information to be distributed in the interest of producing greater cooperation between management and labor; to encourage practice of the Society's code of ethics; and to develop greater appreciation of the personnel function by the general public and management. This third stage conforms to the one proposed by Wilensky.[9]

[8]*ibid.,* pp. 392–393.
[9]Wilensky, "The Professionalization of Everyone?" p. 144.

Personnel has been unable to win the *support of law,* Wilensky's fourth stage of development. One need be neither certified nor licensed to be a personnel administrator.

The national organization and the local chapters of ASPA sponsor meetings and conferences much like those of the earlier personnel associations. In addition, the national has undertaken two unique activities. The first, started in 1951–1952, is the sponsorship of an annual essay contest for college students to encourage writing and research in the personnel field. The second is the development of a code of ethics that regulates both internal relationships (with colleagues) and external relationships (with other members of their organizations, i.e. managers, line officials). This accomplishes the fifth and final stage in Wilensky's sequence: *establishing a regulative code of ethics.*

In its failure to secure licensing or certification for its members and in the failure, until lately, of its training schools to teach a systematic body of theory, personnel as an occupation has yet to achieve professionalism.

The second approach to determine the degree of professionalism of personnel administration is ahistorical. The structural-functionalist school[10] sets forth dimensions that define the "professional model" and personnel administration is examined in terms of its possession of these characteristics. The five defining dimensions are: systematic body of knowledge, rewards, professional authority, service, professional autonomy — colleague control and orientation.

*Systematic body of knowledge*

Unique skills of the "ideal profession" are derived from and supported by a systematic body of theory. The principles that compose this theory describe in general terms the phenomenon with which the professional is concerned. The theory, in turn, is continually verified by application of the scientific method. From the accumulated and verified body of theory "withdrawals can be made as the situation warrants it. . . . The modern professional can trace a specific situation back to theory for a set of specific cause-and-effect relationships."[11] The history of the established professions shows that in the process of expanding their intellectual and theoretical base, from which their

[10]Robert W. Habenstein, "Critique of 'Profession' as a Sociological Category." *Sociological Quarterly,* vol. 4, no. 4 (Autumn 1963), pp. 294–297.

[11]Richard Hall and James D. Thompson, "What do you Mean 'Business is a Profession'?" *Business Horizons,* Spring 1964, p. 40.

technical skill is derived, professionals have emulated the basic biological and physical sciences.

There are problems in describing personnel administration in these terms, and in deciding what technical skills it should require, and from what body of theory these should be derived. Occupations that are organizationally based (like personnel) vary from organization to organization. This lack of agreement on the functions of a personnel administrator and his requisite skills suggests no common pattern of preparation for the occupation. The background of personnel administrators ranges from a college education to on-the-job training; from degrees in law, business administration, personnel, industrial relations, economics to engineering, police administration, or political science.[12] The knowledge base that does exist tends toward the extremes of possessing

> knowledge which is: a) too general or vague [such as unverified theory on "organizational effectiveness"], or b) too narrow and specific. [Until the 1940's, personnel education was technique oriented as witnessed by the plethora of articles about personnel fads, fashions, and gimmicks].[13]

Since the 1940's, however, university scholars and research investigators have devoted a great deal of attention to constructing and testing theories in connection with human problems in working organizations. This field, called "Organizational Behavior," draws on contributions from the behavioral sciences including psychology, sociology, social psychology, and anthropology. It is this alliance with the behavioral sciences, that *may* provide the theoretical basis for personnel's skill in "the human use of human beings,"[14] which has been called its main jurisdiction.

## Rewards

Society's attribution of prestige to an occupation is closely associated with its designation of that occupation as a profession.[15] Occupational prestige rankings are complex evaluations affected by multiple factors. If personnel administration is classified as a profession by workers in

[12]D. H. Kruger, "The Personnel Executive in Quest of Professional Status," *Personnel Administrator*, vol. 6, no. 4 (July–August 1961), p. 18.

[13]Thomas H. Patten, "Is Personnel Administration a Profession?" *Personnel Administration*, vol. 31, no. 2 (March–April 1968), p. 40.

[14]Frank Miller, "Why I'm for Professionalizing," *Personnel Journal*, vol. 38, no. 3 (July–August 1959), pp. 91–94.

[15]Hall and Thompson, p. 40.

the field, one could assume that it is the recipient of high rewards. Wilensky in his article, "The Professionalization of Everyone?" categorizes occupations as established, those in process, borderline, and doubtful.[16] Personnel administration appears in none of these categories, indicating a rather lowly status in terms of societal rewards. The reward associated with professionalism is prestige, although income would be highly, albeit imperfectly, correlated with professionalism. According to the 1968 *Handbook of Labor Statistics*,[17] top paid directors of personnel earn an average of $19,186. In comparison: top paid attorneys, $27,293; top paid engineers, $22,235; top paid engineering technicians, $9,341; top paid other managers, $15,414. If salaries are considered rewards, personnel does not rival the established professions, although it is more highly paid than other professional occupations.

*Professional authority*

A professional's authority is based on his claim to a unique or superior competency in a specialized area of knowledge. Unfortunately, the personnel occupations have only tenuous claims to exclusive expertise. This lack of professional authority results from the newness of the field itself as well as the embryonic state of the behavioral sciences on which personnel draws heavily. In addition, the kinds of problems that personnel deals with are not esoteric. Since everyone believes himself an expert in these areas, he sees no need for specialists in such a field.[18] Despite the gloomy picture of professional authority outlined above, in some of its subareas personnel administrators more closely approximate the professional model. In its staff role, personnel most closely resembles the professional. In this role the personnel administrator offers advice, guidance, and counseling to line officials. One major difference between the personnel administrator and professional in this role is that line officials are not compelled to take the advice they receive. "Nevertheless, like any staff official, the personnel man's authority for specialized help soon becomes accepted if for no other reason than he is a specialist in one particular area."[19]

[16]Harold Wilensky, "The Professionalization of Everyone?" *American Journal of Sociology*, vol. 70, no. 2 (September 1964) p. 142.

[17]U. S. Department of Labor, *Handbook of Labor Statistics* (Washington, D.C.: GPO, 1968).

[18]Wilensky, p. 145.

[19]Heckmann and Huneryager, p. 6.

Thus, although line people do not have to follow personnel's advice, they learn that the personnel administrator's expertise makes it worthwhile to listen. As the line comes to understand the contributions personnel can make, personnel also becomes more familiar with the needs and interests of line managers.[20] This serves further to enhance the professional authority of the personnel administrator.

The personnel administrator also resembles the professional when he performs his role of policy initiator and formulator. On the other hand, in administering "trash-can" services and "directing, coordinating, and controlling employee performance"[21] the personnel administrator exhibits little professional authority.

*Service*

The professional person's responsibility to society is to pursue an occupation largely for others since he has knowledge which is not afforded others. He must carry out his tasks for the benefit of others, placing the client's welfare above his own. If personnel performs a service function, who is the client for the personnel administrator employed by an organization? Is it management, the employees, the customers, or the general public? Since it is difficult to pinpoint personnel's clients, it is also hard to determine whether personnel has adopted a service ideal.

Regarding the service ideal as an institutional pattern, one may ask what are the objectives of large-scale organizations in which personnel administrators are employed? Although profit may be the basic motivation, "social responsibility and the production of goods and services are, of course, indispensable to profit making."[22] The relative emphasis on these objectives will vary from organization to organization, and personnel's behavior in contributing to the accomplishment of these objectives will vary accordingly. In most business organizations, however, profit is given priority. In such an environment it is difficult to identify personnel as service oriented.

*Professional autonomy — colleague control and orientation*

Professional autonomy is evidenced by the pertinent professional association's ability to prescribe standardized programs of academic preparation by licensing and examining practitioners, and by its

[20]Strauss and Sayles, p. 434.
[21]Chruden and Sherman, p. 39.
[22]Patten, p. 41.

ability to promulgate and enforce codes of ethics by censure and expulsion. In the work setting, a professional's autonomy consists of his ability to utilize his skills, to make his own decisions, and to have his work judged only by his professional colleagues. Although national personnel associations hold national and regional meetings, publish journals, and alert members on events in the personnel field, they have not as yet been able to regulate entry into training schools, establish minimum standards of training, examine or license practitioners, or have the power to censure or remove individuals from the occupation. Many personnel people still are developing their skills on the job. The personnel occupation is organizationally based; the organization hires the man for a personnel job, with or without a college degree or a major in personnel, and it may fire him for reasons of its own. Thus the power of the professional association is very limited.

It is also the purpose of the professional association to promulgate and enforce codes of ethics. The codes set up rules concerning the professional's relationships with his clients and with his colleagues. But in attempting to formulate these codes, the personnel associations are faced with the inevitable enigma: Who is the client? There appears to be confusion in the codes as to whether the employees and/or employers of the personnel administrator are his clients. Each personnel administrator may have his own private code of ethics, but if he is bound by a collective code it is that of the organization, not that of an occupational association.[23]

> If the responsibility of staff specialists [personnel administrators] is divided between obligation to the firm that employs him and an association that does not, it is difficult for the association to exert significant control.[24]

In cases where there is conflict between organizational behavior demands and professional codes of ethics, a personnel man who stands firm on the latter, to the point of resignation, probably will have his resignation gladly accepted. Since he serves top management and line supervisors, by whom he is judged and to whom he is ultimately responsible, he cannot be considered professionally autonomous in the work setting.

Contrary, however, to the "occupational myth" of the personnel man as the advisor and recommendation maker with the "velvet touch," this study indicates that personnel men see themselves as independent

[23]Hall and Thompson, p. 43.
[24]*ibid.*, p. 43.

decision makers (see Chapter 5). They feel they do (and should) make independent decisions when confronted with conflict situations. Therefore, it would appear that in one sense, as verified by empirical research, the personnel man is indeed professionally autonomous.

After reviewing these dimensions of the "professional model" and comparing them with the structural dimensions of the personnel occupation, it would appear that, although personnel possesses some of the characteristics found in the "professional model," the personnel occupation still bears but a slight resemblance to a profession.

### Measurement of Individual Professionalism

One measure of individual professionalism is the level of education achieved. Obviously, professional individuals will usually be more highly educated than nonprofessional individuals. The following is the distribution of responding personnel managers by levels of education:

| Education Level | Percentage of Respondents by Highest Level Achieved |
|---|---|
| High school graduate ............... | 4% |
| Some college ...................... | 16 |
| College graduate .................... | 31 |
| Some work toward advanced degree ... | 27 |
| Advanced degree .................... | 22 |

Responding personnel managers are clearly a highly educated group: 80 percent have, at the *minimum*, a college degree; 95 percent have had at least some college education. On the criterion of education, many of the personnel managers studied qualify as professionals. However, examination of other characteristics indicates less professionalism.

Professionals also are likely while in college to major in fields related to their specialty. For personnel managers these academic fields are directly related: behavioral science, business administration, and personnel administration. The following is the distribution of academic majors for college trained personnel managers:

| Major | Percent in Each |
|---|---|
| Behavioral science ......................... | 13% |
| Business administration .................... | 33 |
| Personnel administration ................... | 18 |
| Other ..................................... | 36 |

Slightly less than two-thirds of the respondents had the professional characteristic of majoring in fields related to personnel. The 36 percent who majored in unrelated fields seems high, especially when it is compared with medicine or law where all major in the appropriate academic field.

Professionals are likely to have gone through a process known as sponsorship. In this process someone high in the occupational hierarchy encourages or even offers actual aid to a new entrant. The sponsor, presumably, inculcates the new entrant with a professional ideology. The sponsorship system is particularly common in the established professions of medicine and law. Only 42 percent of the responding personnel managers could single out an individual who had encouraged them to be personnel managers. Slightly more of them (51 percent) had sponsors who offered actual aid. Sponsorship does exist, then, but it is far from universal.

Another characteristic of the professional is planning while still in school for his chosen field. Such planning is necessary in order to have the required specialized education. This pattern is not common in the personnel occupations. Only 34 percent of the responding personnel managers planned to be in personnel while in school.

A related characteristic of the professional is a propensity to enter into the labor market in the chosen field. Doctors, for example, are most likely to begin their careers in medicine. Only 32 percent of the respondents had their first jobs in personnel administration.

Professionals are usually highly active in their major professional association. If a personnel manager is professional, it is hypothesized that he would be most active in ASPA. The following is a summary of the activity of the respondents in various professional associations:

| Professional Association | Number | Mean Number of Years in Each | Mean Activity Level in Each (1-low, 4-high) |
|---|---|---|---|
| ASPA .............. | 349 | 4.8 | 2.3 |
| Other national personnel associations. | 108 | 4.7 | 2.7 |
| Local personnel associations ....... | 262 | 7.3 | 3.0 |
| Nonpersonnel associations ....... | 190 | 6.4 | 2.7 |

Since this was a survey of ASPA members it is not surprising that the largest number of respondents is in ASPA. What is surprising is that the respondents are less active in ASPA than in local personnel associations, nonpersonnel associations, and other national personnel associations. By this criterion many respondents are relatively nonprofessional, since they are not primarily active in their major professional association.

The ethical standards of a professional are typically determined by the professional association. The personnel manager is nonprofessional on this variable, since 7 percent of the respondents felt their ethics were determined by personnel associations.

Professionals are typically highly committed to their occupation, very slightly committed to their employing organization. Personnel managers are committed to both, and only slightly more to their occupation.[25] On a commitment score range of from 5 to 25, the mean occupational commitment for personnel managers was 18.5. The mean organizational commitment score was 18.0. This higher commitment to the occupation was further reflected when the respondents were asked to choose between their company or their occupation. Slightly more than half of the respondents chose their occupation over their company. One would expect a much higher percentage to choose their occupation over their organization in an established profession. Over-all, on the variable of commitment, the responding personnel managers are relatively nonprofessional.[26]

[25]The commitment score computed in this study is treated as an interval scale for statistical purposes. It is recognized, however, that it is not, in reality, an interval scale. We treat it as such so that we can use correlational techniques. Borgatta provides our basic rationale for this approach: "The answer may be imperfect as found, but the task is one of successive approximations. It is not one of avoiding answers because they will not be completely accurate representations of the 'real' relationships....Some parametric estimate is better than no parametric estimate." Borgatta goes on to contend that the use of nonparametric statistics (e.g. Kendall's *tau*) has about an equal number of pitfalls. See E. F. Borgatta, "My Student, the purist; A Lament," *Sociological Quarterly*, vol. 9, 1968, pp. 29–34.

[26]The scores were derived from a series of questions in which the personnel managers were asked if they would definitely change their company (or occupation), are undecided, or definitely not change companies (or occupations), for the following reasons:

1. (a) with no increase in pay
   (b) with a slight increase in pay
   (c) with a large increase in pay

2. (a) with no more freedom
   (b) with little more freedom
   (c) with much more freedom

3. (a) with no more status
   (b) with little more status
   (c) with much more status

4. (a) with no more responsibility
   (b) with little more responsibility
   (c) with much more responsibility

5. (a) with no more opportunity to get ahead
   (b) with little more opportunity to get ahead
   (c) with much more opportunity to get ahead     *(continued)*

Related to present commitment are future goals. The professional is not only presently committed, he also sees himself in that occupation in the future. The following is the breakdown of responding personnel managers by their personal ten-year goals:

| Goals in 10 Years | Percentage Seeing Themselves in Each |
|---|---|
| V.P. of personnel | 37% |
| Personnel manager | 30 |
| Personnel specialist | 2 |
| General management | 22 |
| Other, nonpersonnel positions | 5 |
| Dead, or retired | 4 |

In general, most of the respondents see themselves in personnel in the future. However, a rather large percentage (22 percent) aspire to general management positions, clearly out of the personnel field, a nonprofessional characteristic.

Finally, professional individuals are supposed to be highly mobile. A number of mobility rates were computed in this survey and all indicated that personnel managers were *not* highly mobile. Personnel managers changed companies on the average only once every five years. They changed jobs only slightly more often (1.3 times every five years). Geographically, personnel managers were even less mobile — changing geographical region only about once every ten years. Finally, the responding personnel managers were likely to have worked for only three companies in the course of their careers. On the variable of mobility, personnel managers seem in general to be nonprofessional.

The following summarizes the professional indices used, and the response of the personnel managers studied:

---

Two commitment scores were obtained in this way; commitment to the occupation and commitment to the organization. The commitment score could range from 5 to 25, with the higher score representing a higher degree of commitment. For each of the five groups of factors an individual could get a score from 1 to 5. For example, on the pay factor an individual would be scored as follows: 1. if he would definitely change with no increase in pay; 2. if he would definitely change with a slight increase in pay; 3. if he would definitely change with a large increase in pay; 4. if he is undecided with a large increase in pay; 5. if he would definitely not change with a large increase in pay.

| Professional Indices | The Personnel Manager |
|---|---|
| 1. High degree of education | 1. Highly educated with 95% having at least some college |
| 2. Likely to major, while in college, in personnel or related fields | 2. 64% of the respondents majored in personnel or related fields. |
| 3. Likely to have a sponsor | 3. 42% had a sponsor who encouraged them, while 51% had a sponsor who offered actual aid. |
| 4. Planned to be in occupation while in school | 4. 34% planned to be in personnel while in school. |
| 5. Entry job into the labor force in chosen field | 5. 32% had their first job in personnel. |
| 6. Active in professional association | 6. Less active in their national association (ASPA) than in local personnel groups, other national personnel groups or nonpersonnel associations |
| 7. Ethics determined primarily by professional association | 7. 7% felt that their ethics were determined by personnel associations. |
| 8. High commitment to the occupation | 8. Relatively high percentage committed to their occupation |
| 9. Low commitment to employing organization | 9. Also highly committed to their organization |
| 10. If forced to choose, would choose occupation over organization | 10. 56% chose their occupation over their organization. |
| 11. See themselves in their occupation in the future | 11. 69% see themselves in personnel in 10 years. |
| 12. Highly mobile | 12. On a variety of mobility indices, they exhibit low mobility. |

Clearly, on the evidence of the preceding summary, the individual personnel manager is only mildly professional. He generally has certain professional characteristics (e.g. education, occupational commitment) but, if he aspires to full professionalism, he must concentrate his efforts on many other characteristics.

At both the occupational and individual levels, personnel is lacking in a number of professional characteristics. However, there is a base at both levels upon which to build true professionalism if that is the goal of personnel.

# CHAPTER 4

# Dual Loyalty

THE data on commitment, discussed in the preceding chapter, are somewhat perplexing. Personnel managers are almost as highly committed to their employing organizations as they are to their occupation. This finding is in direct contradiction to what one would expect on the basis of the current theory of commitment.

By organizational commitment, we mean the probability that a person will continue in his organization despite a variety of inducements to leave. Commitment theoretically occurs through a process of placing what Howard Becker calls side bets.[1] When an individual has made a side bet he has "staked something of value to him, something originally unrelated to his present line of activity."[2] Side bets may be made either consciously or unconsciously. Examples of conscious side bets are such actions as investing in stock option plans and the purchasing of a home. "Unconscious commitment arises through a series of acts, no one of which is crucial, but which, taken together, constitute for the actor a series of side bets of such magnitude that he is unwilling to lose them."[3] Unconscious side bets may occur, according to Becker, in a variety of ways: through generalized cultural expectations, by impersonal bureaucratic arrangements, and through the adjustments of the individual to a given social and occupational position. In general, Becker contends that the greater the number of side bets, the greater the commitment of the individual to his organization.

The amount of commitment to the organization of personnel managers was ascertained by a series of questions which attempted to deter-

[1]Howard Becker, "Notes on the Concept of Commitment," *American Journal of Sociology,* vol. 66, 1960, pp. 32–42.
[2]*ibid.,* p. 35.
[3]*ibid.,* p. 38.

mine for what reasons, if any, a person would leave his organization. Such an approach was suggested by Becker in the following statement:

> If, for instance, a person refuses to change jobs, even though the new job offers him a higher salary and better working conditions, we should suspect that his decision is a result of commitment, that other sets of rewards than income and working conditions have become attached to his present job so that it would be too painful for him to change.[4]

He may have a large pension at stake, which he will lose if he moves; he may dread the cost of making new friends and learning to get along with new working associates; he may feel he may get a reputation of being flighty and erratic if he leaves his present job. The dependent variable, organizational commitment, is a score which was computed in much the same way as occupational commitment. (The method of computing these scores is outlined in Chapter 3, n. 26.)

Based primarily on Becker's theory, a number of relationships were hypothesized. It was contended that there was a direct relationship between age and score on commitment to the organization. However, the correlation between age and organizational commitment is .056, a figure which is not significant at the .05 level. The fact that there is no significant relationship between age and organizational commitment casts considerable doubt on Becker's theory of side bets. One of the major components for commitment in Becker's theory is prior actions of the person staking originally extraneous interests on his following a consistent line of activity. It would seem that age would be the best single indicator of the number of such prior actions an individual takes. The older one becomes, the more likely he is to have made a large number of side bets, thereby increasing his commitment to the employing organization. Furthermore, age is, in a sense, itself a side bet. There are in our society, Becker claims, "generalized cultural expectations" which constrain activity. Our society clearly expects older people to be more committed to their organization. Of course, lack of a viable alternative is a further constraint on the older worker. Nevertheless, our society would frown on the idea of a "job-hopping" sixty-year-old. On the other hand, thirty-year-olds in many occupations may be expected to change jobs frequently. Because of the number of side bets and these cultural expectations, one is lead by Becker's theory to expect a positive relationship between age and organizational

[4]Howard Becker, "Personal Change in Adult Life," *Sociometry*, vol. 28, 1964, pp. 50–52.

commitment. The weak correlation reported above is damaging to Becker's theoretical position. Other findings outlined in the next few pages also lend little or no support to the side-bet theory.

It was hypothesized that there was an inverse relationship between education and commitment to the organization. The basic premise supporting this hypothesis is the idea that the less education one has, the fewer the career opportunities open to him, and therefore the greater the number of side bets he must make in the organization employing him. The correlation in this case is in the predicted direction (−.64), but is not statistically significant. This is further evidence that data from the present study do not support the side-bet theory.

Marriage, like old-age and education, should theoretically make one more committed to the employing organization. This view was based on the belief that the married man has greater responsibilities and is, therefore, less willing to lose his investments in the employing organization. The mean organizational commitment score for married respondents is 17.6 (range 5 to 25), while for the unmarried respondents the mean is 18.1. A t-test was performed to determine whether the difference between the means was statistically significant. A t-value of .62 was obtained, which is not statistically significant at the .05 level. This, too, is evidence that the side-bet theory is not supported by the data.

The idea that the more children one has, the more committed one will be to the employing organization is related to the preceding proposition. The result in this case is not only statistically insignificant, it is not even in the predicted direction. The correlation between number of children and organizational commitment is −.026.

The four variables discussed above should, theoretically, be highly related to organizational commitment. That the correlation coefficients are so low for all four would seem to cast doubt on the side-bet theory. Before making any final conclusions about this theory, however, several other supposed correlates of organizational commitment should be examined.

Theoretically, three mobility rates should be related to organizational commitment: rate of intercompany change, rate of job change, and rate of geographic change. Lower rates on these indices were hypothesized to be correlated with high organizational commitment. The rationale behind these hypotheses is that the more committed one is, the greater one's side bets; the less likely one is, therefore, to have risked these investments by making career shifts. The only statistically significant correlation of the three is between rate of intercompany change and organizational commitment. The correlation between these two variables (−.123) is in the predicted direction and, although not very high, is statistically significant at the .05 level. The correlation between organizational commitment and rate of job change is .001. Between organizational commitment and rate of geographical change, the correlation is −.05. Neither correlation is significant at the .05 level.

The basic question to be answered is: Why are all of the correlations between mobility and commitment so low? One of the reasons may be that mobility rates describe past action, while the commitment scores are for the present. The correlation between rate of intercompany change and organizational commitment indicates that there is some relationship between past actions and present commitment. It is difficult to understand why some past actions lead to present commitment while others do not relate. It is possible that the explanation lies in the fact that it takes time to build up enough side bets to be committed to the organization. Since one is unable to change companies while building up side bets, there is a relationship between company changes and present commitment.

The lower correlations for job mobility and geographic mobility may be explained by the same reason. These mobilities are less related to present commitment because one can change jobs and geographic region without changing companies. Hence, job mobility and geographic mobility may be unrelated to organizational commitment. It is possible to have high organizational commitment and also to have high rates of job and geographic change.

It was also hypothesized that *occupational commitment* was inversely related to organizational commitment. The individual who is highly committed to the organization is unlikely to be committed to the occupation. His investment in the employing organization makes him unable to develop a corresponding commitment to the occupation. Data from the present study are strongest on this point, but they are not in the predicted direction. The correlation between the two commitment scores is .320 which is significant at the .05 level. The remarkable conclusion to be drawn is that one who is committed to his organization is also likely to be committed to his occupation.

In general, it may be concluded that all of the preceding statistics indicate that the side-bet theory developed by Becker cannot be supported. It is possible that the lack of theoretical support is caused by some methodological problem in the present study, but it is difficult to see where these errors might be. Rather, it would seem that the theory (organizational commitment arising through a series of side bets) is faulty. One's degree of commitment to the organization may be the result of a variety of factors not considered in Becker's theory. What seems to be needed is a new theory which is capable of accounting for commitment to the organization.

In the side-bet theory, commitment to the organization is a result of a series of positive actions. In that theory, organizational commitment arises through a series of conscious and unconscious side bets. It appears that, on the basis of our knowledge of the personnel occupations, organizational commitment is in reality only a *residual* category. Organizational commitment arises only when the occupation has no really meaningful base to which one may commit himself. The less meaningful the occupation, the more difficult it is for anyone to commit himself to it, and the more likely one is to commit himself to his organization. The basic tenet is that in order to make his work life meaningful, one must commit himself either to his occupation or to his organization. It is possible to be committed to neither occupation nor organization, but it seems that it would be difficult for such an individual to find much satisfaction in his work.

Because of the lack of meaningful content, individuals in society's low status occupations (e.g. clerk) are unlikely to be very committed to their occupations. "The bureaucrat has relatively few skills and is therefore less likely to be involved in his work or identified with his occupation than the professional worker."[5] With very few inducements, individuals in such occupations could be coaxed into another occupation. On the other hand, it is clear "that workers oriented toward their profession are less likely to exhibit a high degree of loyalty to a particular organization than those who are not so oriented."[6] In addition, individuals in society's more prestigious occupations (e.g. doctor, lawyer) are more likely to be committed to their occupations. This high commitment, also, is the result of the meaningful tasks which constitute the occupation. It is difficult, for example, to conceive of an inducement which would cause a doctor to leave his occupation.

This study contends that organizational commitment is basically a psychological phenomenon, not a structural one, as Becker asserts. It arises from a realization by the individual that his occupation offers

---

[5]W. Richard Scott, "Professionals in Bureaucracies: Areas of Conflict" in Howard Vollmer and Donald Mills, eds., *Professionalization* (Englewood Cliffs, N.J.: Prentice-Hall, 1966), p. 274.

[6]*ibid.*

little inducement to commitment. In order to make his work life more meaningful, he must commit himself to something. If the occupation is lacking in content, the organization remains the only work structure to which the individual may commit himself. (A trade union, if it exists, is a third possibility.)

Although the basic process of commitment is psychological, structural factors play an important role at several points. In the first place, the structural attributes of an occupation determine whether or not an individual can commit himself to that occupation. If the structural aspects of the occupation are meaningless, then commitment to it is difficult. In addition, the structural factors discussed by Becker also play a role in organizational commitment. Once an individual has psychologically committed himself to the organization, there are a series of structural constraints which, over time, serve to increase that commitment. These are the side bets Becker has talked about. However, in our theory they are not the major determinants of commitment, they only augment the commitment once it is made psychologically. Examples of such side bets are investment in pension plans and expertise which increasingly is relevant and usable only in the employing organization.

A caveat is in order at this point. The theory of organizational commitment discussed in the preceding pages is extremely hypothetical. It is based on information from one occupation only, the personnel manager. What is needed, obviously, are further studies which attempt to confirm or deny this theory. In order to do this a series of cross-occupational studies, encompassing high- and low-status occupations, is needed.

We have said that, in order to make his work life meaningful, the individual must commit himself either to his organization or to his occupation. Literature on occupational sociology, however, offers another alternative. Several studies have shown that another alternative open to the individual is belief in occupational myth. The development of such myths is not uncommon in low-status occupations. These myths serve the function of enhancing the status of the occupation, at least in the eyes of the individuals involved in the occupation. One example is the psychiatric attendant who views his major responsibility as the care of patients.[7] Another is the night watchman who considers

[7] Richard Simpson and Ida Simpson, "The Psychiatric Attendant: Development of an Occupational Self Image in a Low Status Occupation," *American Sociological Review*, vol. 24, 1959, pp. 389–393.

himself a representative of management.[8] By developing such myths the occupation becomes more palatable and commitment becomes possible. It is unlikely that commitment based on such myths is particularly strong.

The personnel manager seems to retain his commitment to the organization because the occupation is saddled with a large number of meaningless tasks. Functions such as management of janitorial service are still an important part of the personnel function in many companies. The personnel manager, however, has been able to increase his occupational commitment and thereby reduce his organizational commitment because of the increasing number of important tasks assigned to the personnel department. The literature on personnel administration recognizes this tendency. Strauss and Sayles state that recently the influence and prestige of the personnel function have expanded. Thus, with many personnel departments split between meaningful and meaningless tasks, it is not surprising to find the personnel manager committed to both occupation and organization.

The reasons for the dual commitment of personnel managers to both organization and occupation seem to lie in the history of personnel. The personnel occupations have had a checkered history. Two basic concepts dominated the early history of personnel. These have been discussed at length in the first chapter of this study. The first view saw personnel administration as extending welfarism into business. The goal of personnel administration in this view was to make a better life for the employees. Employee counseling which continues to be a typical function of the personnel department is an example of the lingering ideals of welfarism. Another view of personnel administration which remains viable today is the "trash-can" use of the department. That is, functions which no other department wants are assigned to the personnel department. "Plant protection activities (guards), fire-fighting services, in-company telephone services, and reception desk activities — all tend to find their way into the personnel department."[9] A personnel executive summarizes the trash-can view of personnel administration:

> One of the troubles of my company is that they use personnel as a dumping grounds for all kinds of things. We have been kept terrifically busy lately, but a lot of it is stuff that you usually do not find in a personnel department. Every time something comes up that

[8]H. M. Trice, "Night Watchmen: A Study of an Isolated Occupation," *I.L.R. Research,* vol. 10, no. 2, 1960, pp. 3–9.

[9]George Strauss and Leonard Sayles, *Personnel,* 1st ed., pp. 397–398.

they want handled, and they don't know exactly where else to put it, they give it to us. That way I have to spend about half of my time doing things that aren't really the job of the personnel man.[10]

Both the welfare and the trash-can concepts continue to pervade personnel administration.

A new view of personnel administration as a rising profession has begun to grow in recent years. As such it has, in some organizations, been accorded increasing influence and prestige. As we have seen, the personnel occupations have developed a number of structural characteristics of a profession. Personnel administration has become a respectable academic field. Many business schools offer courses in personnel and it is possible to major in personnel administration. Several universities have even established separate schools devoted to personnel administration. In addition, a large number of professional personnel associations have developed at the local and national levels. There is even a movement to unify these disparate groups into one national association. Finally, there is movement toward certification of personnel managers.

It appears that there are three distinct and conflicting views of the nature of personnel administration. We believe that it is the concurrent influence of the three occupational ideologies which enables, *indeed forces,* a personnel manager to be committed to both his occupation and his organization. It would seem that two of the ideologies (welfare and trash-can) lead to organizational commitment. On the other hand, the third ideology (professionalism) enhances occupational commitment.

The trash-can ideology leads to organizational commitment in at least two ways. First, if the personnel manager views his occupation as nothing more than a dumping ground for the organization, it is difficult, if not impossible, for him to develop strong allegiance to his occupation. Unable to commit himself fully to his occupation, the personnel manager must commit himself to the organization in order to make his work life meaningful and satisfactory. Organizational commitment, therefore, arises because the occupation has no real substance with which to identify.

It is possible for the personnel manager to identify in part with his occupation because there is more to it than meaningless tasks. The moderate occupational commitment found in the present study is in recognition of the more worthwhile aspects of the personnel occupa-

[10]*ibid.,* p. 54.

tions. In order, however, to make his work life fully meaningful, the personnel manager is forced to commit himself to both occupation and organization.

Even though the trash-can ideology is no longer acceptable to many personnel managers, it still has an effect on the occupation. In many cases, organizations retain this view of the personnel department, even after personnel managers have abandoned it. Such an organizational view results in a personnel department dominated by unimportant or dull work. The results are the same as if the personnel manager himself believed the department to be the organizational dumping ground — a lack of a meaningful occupation with which to identify and a growing dependence on, and commitment to, the organization.

The welfare view of personnel administration has many of the same effects on the personnel manager, even though it is not as distasteful as the trash-can view. In the welfare ideology, the personnel manager sees himself, and is seen by the organization, as a servant of the employees. He makes no decisions himself, rather he is the advisor to those who seek his counsel. Although such an occupational ideology smacks of martyrdom, it has very little meaningful activity to which a personnel manager may commit himself. Servant of the people may constitute a meaningful occupation for a priest, but it certainly has little status in industry. In an article by Miller and Coghill,[11] this view was associated with the idea that the personnel occupations are, in many ways, feminine occupations. If this view is valid, it is another reason why it is extremely difficult for a man to commit himself to this kind of work. As with the trash-can ideology, the personnel manager who recognizes the welfare aspect of the occupation has little with which to identify. It makes little difference whether the organization, or the individual personnel manager, views personnel administration as a welfare service. If either has this view, the occupation becomes comparatively meaningless. The alternative is commitment to the organization.

Counterbalancing these views of personnel administration is a professional personnel ideology. If either the organization or the individual personnel manager views personnel administration as a profession, there is a strong chance for occupational commitment. Because such a view of personnel administration is gaining recognition, this study revealed some degree of occupational commitment. One of a number of factors affecting the growth of the professional

[11]"Sex and the Personnel Manager," *op. cit.*

ideology in personnel administration is the greater awareness on the part of management of the human factor in industry. Such personnel problems as absenteeism, high personnel costs, increasing unionization, and the need for more skilled workers have enhanced the status of personnel. For the first time, the personnel department emerges as equally important to the organization as the accounting or engineering departments. As human problems in industry have increased, so has the need for expertise in these matters. This has led to the creation of special courses, even special schools, designed to teach people how to deal with these problems. This gives personnel managers, for the first time, a specialized body of knowledge which further enhances their status in the organization. As the abilities of personnel managers grow, important new functions are assigned to their department. In addition, many of the meaningless chores are either moved elsewhere or made into an insignificant part of the department's activities. With these changes taking place, it is easy to see why it is now possible for the personnel manager to become committed to his occupation.

All three of these ideologies, trash-can, welfare, and professional, exist today in the personnel occupations. It is their coexistence which does much to explain many of the findings in the present study. For example, the presence of these ideologies helps to explain the coexistence of occupational and organizational commitment. Since personnel managers are affected by all three ideologies, they are naturally split in their allegiance. Lingering trash-can and welfare ideologies lead toward organizational commitment. Emerging professionalization pulls in the other direction, toward occupational commitment. Because the personnel manager sees himself, and others view him, in all three roles, a dual commitment is able to exist.

This dual commitment is perpetuated by forces which continue to pull the personnel manager in both directions. One view which keeps him committed to the organization is that personnel administration involves no real expertise and that consequently anyone can do the job. Other factors tug the personnel manager in the direction of occupational commitment; for example, the increasing number of schools and institutes of industrial relations, the growth of professional personnel associations, and a growing body of personnel theory.

In sum, the case of the personnel manager illustrates our theory of organizational commitment. The occupation as a whole is only partially meaningful; therefore personnel managers are only moderately committed to it. To make his work life meaningful, the personnel manager must supplement his commitment to the occupation with some degree of organizational commitment.

# CHAPTER 5

# Behavior in Role Conflict Situations

OVER half of the nationwide mail questionnaire was devoted to two role conflict cases. The purpose was to determine how personnel managers resolve such conflicts. Theoretically, this portion of the study was designed to retest and supplement the basic theory of role conflict resolution as developed by Gross, Mason, and McEachern,[1] based on their study of the school superintendent. Gross and his associates hypothesized that there were four alternative means of resolving role conflict: (1) conform to expectation A; (2) conform to expectation B; (3) attempt to conform in part to both expectations by some compromise behavior; (4) avoid conforming to either of the expectations, (withdrawal).

Gross and his associates believed that they could predict which of these means an individual would select to resolve role conflict. The first factor used in prediction was legitimacy, or the *right* others have to expect the focal role to behave in conformity with their expectations. Their second factor was the ability of significant others[2] to *sanction* the focal role for nonconformity to their expectations. The third factor was a personality variable which predisposes an individual to

---

[1]Neal Gross, Ward S. Mason, Alexander W. McEachern. *Explorations in Role Analysis: Studies of the School Superintendency Role* (New York: John Wiley, 1958).

[2]The term "significant others," used throughout the study, means persons in other positions within the organization with whom the personnel manager has contact and whom he considers to be important sources of advice.

give primacy to either legitimacy or sanctioning ability. They believed that individuals would have one of three distinct personality orientations in a role conflict situation. The first was a moral orientation in which the individual tends to emphasize legitimacy and minimize sanctioning ability. The second was an expedient orientation in which the focal role emphasizes sanctioning ability over legitimacy. In the third type, the moral expedient, the individual sees a net balance between sanctioning ability and legitimacy. On the basis of the ratings of significant others on legitimacy and sanctioning ability and knowledge of the individual's orientation, Gross was able to predict 264 of 291 conflict resolutions correctly.[3]

These impressive results led to a series of follow-up studies which did little more than retest some of the ideas developed by Gross and his associates.[4] They added little to the basic theoretical orientation. The present study was designed to supplement the theory of role conflict resolution as it currently stands.

In the mail questionnaire, two cases were presented to the respondents. The first case read:

> Several weeks ago a terrible storm hit your area. Because of the storm, a number of employees at your location were unable to work. The employees involved were not in a union. This is the first time such a situation has occurred at your location and there is no policy or precedent on handling such an issue. You have thought over the situation and decided that there are good arguments for both paying and not paying the employees for time lost. Although you are now undecided, you have sought advice from significant figures in your organization. Your recommendation will be based solely on the advice you receive in each case.

Four significant figures are involved in the case: (1) the manager of the accounting department; (2) the man immediately above you in the personnel department; (3) the top company official at your location; (4) your immediate subordinate whose knowledge will be relevant to this situation.

Following the case were the following six situations:

1. The man immediately above you in the personnel department

---

[3]*ibid.*, p. 305.

[4]See, for example, Delbert Miller and Fremont Shull. "The Prediction of Administrative Role Conflict Resolutions," *Administrative Science Quarterly*, vol. 7, 1962, pp. 143–160; Alvin Magid, "Dimensions of Administrative Role and Conflict Resolution Among Local Officials in Northern Nigeria," *Administrative Science Quarterly*, vol. 12, 1967, pp. 321–338.

is in favor of paying for the time lost, but the top company official at your location is opposed.

2. The manager of the accounting department is in favor of paying for the time lost, but the man immediately above you in the personnel department is opposed.

3. The top company official at your location is in favor of paying for the time lost, but the manager of the accounting department is opposed.

4. The manager of the accounting department is in favor of paying for the time lost, but your immediate subordinate whose knowledge would be relevant to the situation is opposed.

5. Your immediate subordinate is in favor of paying for the time lost, but the top company official at your location is opposed.

6. Your immediate subordinate is in favor of paying for the time lost, but the man immediately above you in the personnel department is opposed.

After each situation, the personnel manager had five alternative choices which represent the four developed by Gross and his associates and our addition of a fifth alternative of independent action (operationally defined as "listen to both but make your own recommendation"):

1. Recommend pay for the time lost (expectation A).
2. Do not recommend pay for the time lost (expectation B).
3. Talk to the two parties and attempt to resolve their differences (compromise).
4. Listen to both, but make your own recommendation (independent action).
5. Hold your recommendation in abeyance (withdrawal).

In addition, a second case was included which read as follows:

An outside consultant was hired some months ago by your company to study the personnel department. He has just submitted his report and, among other things, it recommends several changes in the duties assigned to you. You see both merits and failings in the suggested changes. On the whole, therefore, you are undecided on whether the company should accept the recommendations for change. Although you are now undecided, you have been told that you must make a recommendation. Since you are undecided, you have sought advice from significant figures in your organization. Your decision will be based solely on the advice you receive in each case.

The same significant figures were involved in Case 2 as were in Case 1. The six situations for Case 2 are the same as Case 1 except, instead of significant figures making recommendations for or against paying for the time lost, their recommendations are for or against the proposed changes. After each situation, the respondent had the same basic alternatives as in each of the situations in Case 1.

One of our basic hypotheses was that in the role conflict situation, the independent choice of action which we added to the Gross scheme was as likely to be chosen as any of the other behavioral alternatives. Tables 1 and 2 present the findings which relate to this hypothesis.

*Table 1.* Distribution of Behavioral Choices for Each Situation in Case 1.

| Behavioral Alternatives | Situations | | | | | |
|---|---|---|---|---|---|---|
| | *1* | *2* | *3* | *4* | *5* | *6* |
| Conform to expectation A... | 69 | 38 | 127 | 42 | 49 | 36 |
| Conform to expectation B... | 26 | 72 | 13 | 29 | 58 | 42 |
| Compromise............... | 137 | 108 | 83 | 61 | 59 | 120 |
| Independent action......... | 156 | 170 | 175 | 265 | 229 | 191 |
| Withdraw................ | 6 | 4 | 2 | 1 | 5 | 3 |

*Table 2.* Chi² Values in Case 1 for Independent Action Paired with the Next Most Frequently Chosen Alternative in Each Situation.

| Situations—Case 1 | Chi² Values |
|---|---|
| 1................................................... | 1.2 |
| 2................................................... | 13.8* |
| 3................................................... | 7.6* |
| 4................................................... | 127.6* |
| 5................................................... | 100.3* |
| 6................................................... | 16.2* |

*Represents a Chi² value statistically significant at the .05 level.

It is clear from Table 1 that the hypothesis on independent action is affirmed. More surprising is the fact that independent action is the most frequently chosen behavioral alternative in every situation in Case 1. Chi-square tests were performed to determine whether the differences between independent action and the next most frequently chosen alternative were statistically significant. All but one of the six Chi-square values is statistically significant at the .05 level. As has been discussed, this reveals a severe limitation on the theory of role conflict resolution developed by Gross, Mason, and McEachern.

A criticism may be made that these findings are unrealistic. It may be that it is only in the safe and unreal world of the questionnaire that a personnel manager dares to take independent action. Although this is a powerful argument, there is a good deal of evidence that it is not true. In the first place, pretest, open-ended interviews indicated that such an action was selected by personnel managers in the real world. Second, evidence from the interview portion of this study, which was open-ended, supports these findings. Of the fifty subjects classified, twenty were typified by a reliance on authority or power in arriving at the solution of a problem. There are a number of other supports for this argument and this discussion will be pursued at length in the concluding chapter of this study.

The findings for Case 2 exhibit the same, even stronger, tendency for independent action to be the most frequently chosen behavioral alternative. Tables 3 and 4 illustrate this point.

Table 3. Distribution of Behavioral Choices for Each Situation in Case 2.

| Behavioral Alternatives | Situations | | | | | |
|---|---|---|---|---|---|---|
| | 1 | 2 | 3 | 4 | 5 | 6 |
| Conform to expectation A... | 42 | 17 | 123 | 22 | 32 | 22 |
| Conform to expectation B... | 18 | 79 | 5 | 31 | 44 | 34 |
| Compromise............... | 97 | 48 | 40 | 46 | 51 | 107 |
| Independent action......... | 228 | 240 | 223 | 293 | 259 | 227 |
| Withdraw................. | 7 | 9 | 4 | 2 | 9 | 3 |

Table 4. Chi$^2$ Values in Case 2 for Independent Action Paired with the Next Most Frequently Chosen Alternative in Each Situation.

| Situations—Case 2 | Chi$^2$ Values |
|---|---|
| 1...................................................... | 52.8* |
| 2...................................................... | 81.3* |
| 3...................................................... | 28.9* |
| 4...................................................... | 181.1* |
| 5...................................................... | 139.5* |
| 6...................................................... | 43.1* |

*Represents a Chi$^2$ value statistically significant at the .05 level.

In Case 2, as in Case 1, independent action is the most frequently chosen behavioral alternative. In addition, the differences between independent action and the next most frequently chosen alternative are statistically significant in every situation.

A number of interesting implications can be drawn from the preceding findings. Of central importance is what these findings suggest to us about other occupations. We have discovered in preceding chapters that the personnel occupations are not particularly professional. If such a relatively nonprofessional occupation is prone to taking independent action, then one might expect the more professional occupation to exhibit an even greater tendency toward independence in a role conflict situation.

There is another interesting implication of the findings on independent action. In the pretest interviews, a number of personnel managers indicated that they were *not* decision-makers but were primarily advisors. As a matter of fact, many of them thought that the role conflict cases would not be meaningful because almost everyone would choose the compromise resolution. However, it has been shown that independent action *is* by far the most frequently chosen alternative. Obviously, there is a wide gap between what personnel managers believe they would do in a role conflict situation and what they say they do. The occupational ideology is at variance with practice. It is clear that there is a mythical image of personnel operating in this instance. It is to this mythical image that the last chapter devotes much of its discussion.

There are a number of other interesting findings in Tables 1 and 3. First of all, compromise in almost every situation is the second most popular behavioral alternative. Withdrawal is chosen so infrequently as to indicate that it may not be a viable alternative in a role conflict situation. Finally, it is clear in Tables 1 and 3 that whether one conforms to expectation A or B varies with the situation and is determined by a variety of factors involved in each situation. These factors are discussed later in this chapter.

Two cases were included in order to assess consistency of resolution of conflict. Table 5 shows that a number of differences exist between cases in the way role conflict is resolved.

A number of interesting conclusions may be drawn from Table 5:

1. Independent action is chosen more frequently, in every situation, in Case 2. However, in only three of the six situations is this difference statistically significant.

2. The least difference between the two cases on independent action occurs in situation 4 where the two least powerful significant others are paired. Because of the impotence of these two significant others, independent action is chosen very frequently in spite of the differences in the issue. The weakness of the significant others makes the nature of the issue of secondary importance.

3. The greatest difference between the two cases on independent

Table 5. A Comparison of the Two Role Conflict Cases.

| Situation 1 | Case 1 | Case 2 |
|---|---|---|
| Conform to expectation A | 69 | 42 |
| Conform to expectation B | 26 | 18 |
| Compromise | 137 | 97 |
| Independent action | 156 | 228 |
| Withdraw | 6 | 7 |

| Situation 2 | Case 1 | Case 2 |
|---|---|---|
| Conform to expectation A | 38 | 17 |
| Conform to expectation B | 72 | 79 |
| Compromise | 108 | 48 |
| Independent action | 170 | 240 |
| Withdraw | 4 | 9 |

| Situation 3 | Case 1 | Case 2 |
|---|---|---|
| Conform to expectation A | 127 | 123 |
| Conform to expectation B | 13 | 5 |
| Compromise | 83 | 40 |
| Independent action | 175 | 223 |
| Withdraw | 2 | 9 |

| Situation 4 | Case 1 | Case 2 |
|---|---|---|
| Conform to expectation A | 42 | 22 |
| Conform to expectation B | 29 | 31 |
| Compromise | 61 | 46 |
| Independent action | 265 | 293 |
| Withdraw | 1 | 2 |

| Situation 5 | Case 1 | Case 2 |
|---|---|---|
| Conform to expectation A | 49 | 32 |
| Conform to expectation B | 58 | 44 |
| Compromise | 59 | 51 |
| Independent action | 229 | 259 |
| Withdraw | 5 | 9 |

| Situation 6 | Case 1 | Case 2 |
|---|---|---|
| Conform to expectation A | 36 | 22 |
| Conform to expectation B | 42 | 34 |
| Compromise | 120 | 107 |
| Independent action | 191 | 227 |
| Withdraw | 3 | 3 |

action occurs in situation 1 where the two most powerful significant others are paired. It appears that the nature of the issue has a greater impact on the resolution of role conflict when the focal role is confronted with two powerful significant others. In Case 2, where the personnel manager's job is at stake, he is more likely to ignore the significant others and take independent action. The nature of the issue, in Case 2, is important enough to make the personnel manager more likely to challenge the authority of powerful significant others.

4. Another conclusion that may be drawn from Table V is the decreased likelihood of compromise in Case 2. This, too, may be attributed to the nature of the issue. In Case 2, with his job at stake, the personnel manager is less likely to be a compromiser. The differences for compromise in the two cases is, as for independent action, statistically significant in only three of the six situations.

5. On the behavioral alternative of conforming to the expectations of significant other A, the least difference between the two cases occurs in situation 3. In this situation, the powerful top company official is paired with the weak accounting manager. In such a situation, the nature of the issue appears to be unimportant and the decision made is dictated by the power of the top company official.

6. The differences between the two cases is greatest, on conforming to the expectations of significant other A, in situation 2 where the two weakest significant others are paired. Twice as many respondents in Case 1 are likely to agree with the accounting manager, significant other A, as do in Case 2. Here the nature of the issue is of overriding importance. The accounting manager is less potent in Case 2 because, unlike Case 1, money is not the issue. In addition, the issue in Case 2 is more of an internal personnel matter and this further reduces the importance of the accounting manager.

7. The greatest difference, on conforming to the expectation of significant other B, occurs in situation 5. In situation 5, the immediate subordinate is paired with the top company official. The top company official, significant other B, is less influential in Case 2. One possible explanation may be the fact that the issue in Case 2 is more of an internal personnel matter in which the top company official would not be involved.

It was also hypothesized that, when the personnel manager is confronted with a situation in which a more powerful significant other is paired with a less powerful significant other, he is more likely to resolve the conflict in favor of the more powerful significant other. Table 6 outlines the relevant results of this hypothesis (see page 54).

In nine of the twelve situations, results are in the predicted direction. In only four of the nine, however, are the differences statistically significant. At best, the hypothesis is only mildly supported. Only situations 2 and 3 in both cases strongly support the hypothesis. In situation 2, the manager of the accounting department is paired with

Table 6. Distribution of Resolutions in Favor of More Powerful and Less Powerful Significant Other with Chi² Values for Each of the Differences between the Two Distributions.

| Case | Situation | Resolution in Favor of the More Powerful Significant Other | Resolution in Favor of the Less Powerful Significant Other | $Chi^2$ |
|------|-----------|------------------------------------------------------------|-----------------------------------------------------------|---------|
| 1........ | 1 | 26 | 69 | 19.5* |
|  | 2 | 72 | 38 | 10.5* |
|  | 3 | 127 | 13 | 92.8* |
|  | 4 | 42 | 29 | 2.4 |
|  | 5 | 58 | 49 | .8 |
|  | 6 | 42 | 36 | .5 |
| 2........ | 1 | 18 | 42 | 9.6* |
|  | 2 | 79 | 17 | 40.0* |
|  | 3 | 123 | 5 | 108.8* |
|  | 4 | 22 | 31 | 1.5 |
|  | 5 | 44 | 32 | 1.9 |
|  | 6 | 34 | 22 | 2.6 |

*Represents a Chi² value statistically significant at the .05 level.

the respondent's immediate superior. In both cases, there was a very pronounced tendency to conform to the expectation of the immediate superior. This confirms the hypothesis since the accounting manager is less powerful than the immediate superior. Furthermore, the gap between the immediate superior and the accounting manager on power is very large.

In situation 3, the accounting manager is paired with the most powerful significant other, the top company official. It is in this situation that there is the greatest tendency to resolve in favor of the more powerful significant other.

The other situations also tend to support the hypothesis but do so less clearly. In situation 5, in both cases, the most and least powerful significant others are paired. It is in this situation that one would expect the greatest tendency to resolve in favor of the more powerful significant other. However, the discrepancy in this situation is not as great as in situations 2 and 3, although it is in the predicted direction. This seems to suggest that there are factors other than power which determine whether a personnel manager will resolve role conflict in favor of one significant figure or the other. This point will be picked up again later.

Situation 1, in both cases, is theoretically puzzling. The differences are statistically significant, but not in the predicted direction. In situation 1, the man immediately above in the personnel department is paired with the top company official. These are the two most powerful significant others with the top company official being ranked slightly more powerful than the immediate superior. In theory, the respondent should resolve in favor of the top company official, but the results are in the opposite direction. Once again, the answer seems to lie in the fact that there are factors other than power which determine the potency of the significant other.

The respondents were asked to make a series of rankings of the significant others involved in the cases on five variables: power, legitimacy, visibility, expertise, and friendliness. When one looks at the combined rankings for all five factors, one finds that in many cases it is a combined score on these five variables which determine the potency of a significant order rather than just his power ranking. Other findings seem to support the idea that there are a number of variables which determine the potency of a significant other. For instance, in situation 3, there is a very strong tendency to resolve in favor of the top company official. Considering only power, this is not surprising since the top company official is ranked first on power and the accounting manager is ranked third. Yet, if power was the determining factor, one would expect an even stronger tendency to resolve in favor of the top company official when he is paired with a figure who is ranked lowest on power, the immediate subordinate. This pairing occurs in situation 5 where there is a tendency to resolve in favor of the top company official, but this trend is much less pronounced than in situation 3. This is further evidence that factors other than power help to determine a significant other's potency.

It was also hypothesized that personnel managers are more likely to compromise when the two most powerful significant others are paired than in any other situation. Table 7 summarizes the findings on this factor. Nine of the ten pairings in the table exhibit differences which are in the predicted direction. In seven of those nine pairings, the Chi-square values are statistically significant. In both cases, situation 6 is an exception to the hypothesis. In that situation, the figures paired are superior and subordinate in the personnel department. It seems logical to conclude that the personnel manager is prone to compromise in this situation because both significant others are in his department. Because they are both in his department, the personnel manager feels it more convenient and more necessary to compromise. As a matter of fact, this factor is so important that situation 6 attracts

Table 7. Number of Compromise Choices in Each Situation with Chi² Tests between the Situation in Which the Two Most Powerful Significant Others Are Paired and the Other Five Situations.

| Case | Situation | No. of Compromise Choices | Chi² |
|------|-----------|---------------------------|------|
| 1.................. | **1 | 137 | — |
| | 2 | 108 | 3.4 |
| | 3 | 83 | 13.3* |
| | 4 | 61 | 29.2* |
| | 5 | 59 | 31.0* |
| | 6 | 120 | 1.1 |
| 2.................. | **1 | 97 | — |
| | 2 | 48 | 16.6* |
| | 3 | 40 | 23.7* |
| | 4 | 46 | 18.2* |
| | 5 | 51 | 14.3* |
| | 6 | 107 | .5 |

*Represents a Chi² value significant at the .05 level.
**Situation in which two most powerful significant others are paired.

more compromise choices in the second case than a situation in which the two most powerful significant others are paired.

Situation 2, in Case 1, also attracts a large number of compromise resolutions. This is not so in situation 2, in Case 2. In situation 2, the accounting manager is paired with the immediate superior in personnel. The nature of the issue seems to account for differences between the two cases in situation 2. Since Case 1 involves a monetary issue, the personnel manager accords the accounting manager greater status. Because of this, the personnel manager is more likely to compromise between the accounting manager and his immediate superior in personnel in Case 1. In the second case, no money is involved so the importance of the accounting manager declines. Due to the decreased potency of the accounting manager, the personnel manager finds it less necessary to compromise in the second situation of Case 2.

A final hypothesis was that personnel managers are more likely to take independent action when the two least powerful significant others are paired than in any other situation. The results applicable to the preceding hypothesis are shown in Table 8.

Table 8 strongly confirms the hypothesis that independent action is more likely when the personnel manager is confronted with the two weakest figures than in any other situation. All but two of the Chi-square values are statistically significant.

*Table 8.* Number of Independent Actions Elected in Each Situation with Chi² Tests between the Situation in Which the Two Least Powerful Significant Others Are Paired and the Other Five Situations.

| Case | Situation | No. of Independent Actions | Chi² |
|------|-----------|----------------------------|------|
| 1................... | 1 | 156 | 28.2* |
| | 2 | 170 | 20.7* |
| | 3 | 175 | 18.4* |
| | **4 | 265 | — |
| | 5 | 229 | 2.5 |
| | 6 | 191 | 12.0* |
| 2................... | 1 | 228 | 10.4* |
| | 2 | 240 | 5.3* |
| | 3 | 223 | 9.5* |
| | **4 | 293 | — |
| | 5 | 259 | 2.1 |
| | 6 | 227 | 8.4* |

*Represents a Chi² value significant at the .05 level.
**Situation in which two least powerful significant others are paired.

Of primary importance in this chapter is the finding that the personnel manager is, indeed, an independent actor. Although his propensity toward independent action varies with situations and who is involved in those situations, the over-all finding confirms the fact that he behaves independently both in superior-subordinate relations and in other types of conflict situations. The point has been raised before that this is at variance with the occupational image of the personnel manager. It is to this gap between the occupational image and the findings of the study which the concluding chapter of this book addresses itself.

# CHAPTER 6

# Conflict Resolution:

# Interview Data

THE question of validity inevitably arises in studies of this kind. Does evidence from another source, arrived at by different research methods used on the same question, indicate the same trends? This chapter on the interview portion of this study and the following chapter devoted to an analysis of a single company offer support for the preceding findings. (See Appendix C for the interview schedule.)

Interviews were conducted in New York City, Syracuse, Rochester, Buffalo, and Cleveland, Ohio. The choice of cities was based mainly on availability of respondents. No attempt was made to have a representative group in statistical terms, although all personnel managers fulfilled the two basic requirements: (a) that they be the personnel executives in charge of industrial relations in their locations; and (b) that they have a staff of specialists reporting to them. Several of the respondents worked at the corporate level and some at the division level. The majority, however, were individuals in charge of the personnel activity at the plant or local level. The actual distribution by levels of interviewees was:

Vice-presidents, corporate level ........................... 6
Directors of industrial relations, division level .............. 15
Managers of industrial relations, plant level ................ 29

Total ..................................... 50

Approximately 50 percent of the group interviewed were members of ASPA; the rest had local affiliations. No differences in cooperation were noted between the ASPA members and nonmembers. Six of those interviewed were female personnel executives. The interviews were tape-recorded, except for the few who objected and those were recorded in long hand.

The interview schedule had several sections. One was on demographic data related to the academic and work background of the respondent: his educational level, his major in college, his work experience, and his age. Essentially the same type of information was obtained from him about his subordinates. Data were also obtained on the nature, size, and structure of the organization.

The primary focus of the interview schedule was on superior-subordinate conflict. The exact phrasing of the main question in this part was: "Please describe for me, in as much detail as possible, a situation in which you and one of your subordinates have held dissenting views on an issue related to the work activity." While the personnel manager was relating the situation, the interviewer made sure that he covered eight major points: the nature of the issue; the manner in which it developed; persons involved; positions taken by each party; action taken towards solution; alternative solutions, if any; persons having the final say and why; the final outcome of the situation.

In addition to this type of conflict situation, information was gathered on two other experiences: a situation in which the respondents were faced with conflicting expectations of them by two significant figures in the organization; and a situation of conflict between themselves and one other significant figure in line operating management. In both these situations, the same eight points were probed.

The personnel managers were requested to describe actual situations rather than hypothetical ones. Free choice of recollection was an objective; direction was given only when the respondent strayed off the topic or had not covered the points on the check list.

It was apparent from the tapes and interview notes that there were four basic types of personnel administrators according to their approaches to resolving conflict with their subordinates: (a) the one who relies on his power or authority to resolve the conflict; (b) the one who seeks a compromise between his position and the position taken by the subordinate; (c) the one who, although he differs with his subordinate, allows the subordinate to follow his inclination; (d) the one who refuses to resolve the conflict and "passes the buck" to a third party for a decision. Placing a particular respondent in one category or another was necessarily a subjective decision. The key was in the answer to the question of how the conflict was resolved. Since the bulk of the interviews was taped, it was possible to go over the responses with great care. In most instances the decision was easy; the statements clearly fitted a type. There were, however, borderline instances which were decided after close examination of the attitude and style of the final approach taken by the manager.

The first type is the authority-wielder, or the personnel manager who in this study relied on authority or power to arrive at the solution of a problem. He was the one who did not permit his subordinate a dissenting view in decision-making. He issued a directive to the subordinate with whom he was in conflict, permitting little or no compromise between their positions. This approach was exemplified by such remarks as: "My subordinate is a pretty mature individual. He accepts the premise that, after having his day in court and after having talked it out, he accepts the authority of my position." "If I can't persuade my subordinate to do what I recommend, then I make a decision and he has two alternatives: he may do it, or he may leave." "In a conflict with my training director, George, he proves to be quite occasionally inflexible, which means that I have to say sometimes: 'George, as your boss, I am pulling this guy out' and I have to do this arbitrarily." This domination strategy forces compliance; he is using the authority of his position to resolve the conflict.

Of the fifty personnel managers interviewed, twenty (40 percent) took this approach. This, then, was the most frequently used single tactic by the group studies. There were, however, some variations in this classification. All individuals did not follow the hard-line approach. Different ways of exercising authority ranged from the extreme cases described above to milder forms of reliance on power such as the suggestive approach. The fact that this type predominated is consistent with the prevalence in the national survey of the type of personnel manager whose style is primarily that of independent decision-maker.

Comparison with the other three types showed that the authority-wielders were significantly older and had predominantly labor relations backgrounds. This seems to indicate that experienced personnel managers tend to rely more on authority when resolving conflict with subordinates. In addition, since in the history of the personnel occupations labor relations emerged as the personnel occupation with the greatest amount of expertise, this background further conditioned occupants of this personnel occupation toward authoritative style.

Personnel managers in the second group were classified as compromisers. Ten of the fifty managers were so classified. These superiors gave their subordinates a sense of participating in the decision-making. They tended to agree with the subordinate's position on an issue, discussed it with him, and instead of imposing their way or issuing an order, offered a solution to which they both had contributed. Three comments by compromisers illustrate this position: "I usually like to resolve conflicts with subordinates at the lowest level possible. It is also important that in solving the problem we have agreement.... I feel it is vital that we see eyeball to eyeball. We can't solve a problem if he is well entrenched in his position. A manager must never lose sight of the fact that it is his end responsibility to his boss and to his company. He can't shake it off or wash his hands of that responsibility. I think it is important that in the solution of a conflict we have good rapport in boss-subordinate relationship; that they be able to tell me: 'Boy, you sure made a goof on that one. It'll never fly.' They know they can say that to me and I'll take it in the right spirit. I can say much the same thing and they will respect it."

"When my subordinates and I discuss a matter related to their function we sit down and sort of throw rank out of the window. We are equals then."

"I would never impose my position on a subordinate when we have a conflict. He is usually an expert in his field and he might have looked at some aspects which I have overlooked. The process of supervision is not that clear; I can't tell a man to do something he doesn't want to do. We have to sit down and see the pros and cons of each position. In this case he suggested a compromise position which was clearly viable to me."

These supervisors engaged in a consultative relationship with their subordinates. They felt that their subordinates' ideas could not be entirely wrong and searched for the valid points in them.

The third classification was typified by delegation of decision to the subordinate. There were four of these out of the total of fifty interviewees. These were supervisors who, even though they were in disagreement, would give their subordinates the freedom to follow their own course if they felt strongly that it was adequate for the solution of the conflict. This is a form of delegation extended to a maximum degree. Two of them commented as follows:

"I built a group of top flight specialists; men who could master their own activities without constant help on my part. I can't pretend to be knowledgeable in all areas of management and manpower. I feel that, as a supervisor, my job is to coordinate the activities of my men. I couldn't tell them what to do because, as I said, I don't know everything that goes on down there. . . . Why, I would be President of the U.S. if I knew so much. So, I give them complete freedom of decision, even when we disagree. I have to trust their judgment as experts."

"You have to give your subordinates enough responsibility and power to develop them as human beings. Delegation is conducive to better performance because the man feels he is trusted. As long as my men are doing what their responsibilities call for I don't need to direct them. I can be out of this office and I know everything will run smoothly."

The final classification into which respondents were placed was, in effect, the buck-passer. This group was the second largest — sixteen out of fifty. These were personnel managers who submitted the issue of conflict with a subordinate to a third party for solution. Therefore, they "passed the buck" to someone else and withdrew from solving the problem themselves. This approach was exemplified by such remarks as:

"In any of the major issues that my subordinates feel strongly enough, they ought to have a voice with the president of the company as well as with myself. Sometimes, when we do not come to an agreement, I tell my subordinate: 'All right, I can accept your way if you accept my way. Let's go to the president and see what he thinks about it.' "

"It all depends upon how strong my subordinate's position is. If I can't convince him of my point of view, usually we submit the issue to my boss, so that he may serve as a catalyst. It would be short-sighted on my part to force my point of view down his throat if I want him to remain around here."

It is clear that a surprising number of personnel managers were classified as authority-wielders but to determine the validity of this finding it was compared with the results of the other two conflict situations. Recall that these two were: (a) conflictive situation in which they were called upon to make a decision by the two persons who had conflicting views of what he should do; (b) a situation in which they were personally in conflict with line operating managers. In order to give a broader perspective to this study, we asked the respondents to supply us with their version of these two additional conflict situations. Our purpose was to determine whether there was, or was not, consistency in the style in which the personnel manager resolved the three different conflict situations. Of the twenty "authority-wielders," fifteen were considered consistent, while five were inconsistent. Of the ten "compromisers," only three were consistent, while seven were inconsistent. Of the four "delegators," three of these were classified as consistent. Finally, only two of the sixteen "buck-passers" were classified as consistent, the other fourteen were inconsistent.

The authority-wielders, then, were apparently the most consistent of the four groups. The compromisers showed little consistency which suggests that these individuals are flexible, even unpredictable, in their behavior. The four delegators were generally consistent, while the sixteen buck-passers were mostly inconsistent.

These findings on authority use are of paramount importance. They are opposed to what most personnel texts assume and personnel people believe. At the same time, they are consistent with the national survey of members of the ASPA. One caution is necessary, however, since a second trend appears also; the buck-passer and compromiser are quite prominent in these studies. Even though the professional trend is present, as exemplified by the many independent authority-wielders, the more traditional helper-adviser and trash-can situation is still very much in evidence.

In sum, there is evidence to support the belief that there is a trend which will probably grow, toward a professionally oriented type of personnel manager. At the same time, the widely held belief that he is a "politician" is far from untrue. The occupation will probably continue to reflect these diverse aspects for some time.

CHAPTER 7

# Role of the Personnel
# Department: A Case Study

THE data in the preceding chapters came either from the national survey or from studies of a number of personnel administrators in many companies in several cities of New York and Ohio. The case study discussed in this chapter, on the other hand, is of one large industrial organization. These data were collected not by the authors but by researchers in the organization itself and were submitted as part of a report to their top management. Much of it is so relevant to the other studies that it is presented here to supplement and highlight the other findings. Since we did not have any control over the study, we cannot attest to its methodological soundness. Despite this caveat, the following data are presented to reinforce our previous discussions.

Interviews were conducted in this organization with one hundred forty-seven preselected members of management. These interviews had two major purposes: (a) to obtain perceptions regarding the problems within the personnel management function, and (b) to obtain ideas for improving the function.

The interviews were conducted by management consultants and selected personnel people appointed to a task force to do the study. The interviews were carried out on several organizational levels: at the *corporate level* — most officers, including all members of the corporate policy committee, most functional department heads, and all key managers of the corporate personnel department; at the *division level* — all general managers, all personnel managers, and selected managers of a variety of other functional departments; at the *plant level* — many of the plant managers, and most of their immediate subordinates; also, selected managers from other company centers.

Questionnaires, sent to all people in personnel, had the following foci: the activities they perform; the amount of time they spend on each activity; the emphasis placed on various personnel activities; trends and problems they perceive; ideas they have for improving the function.

The report by the company task force identified problems and solutions in a number of areas: the way personnel policies are decided upon and carried out; the way the role of the personnel function is presently defined; the professional skills of the people in the function; the structure of the personnel function.

The task force found that the role of the personnel department in their organization was not clearly defined. There was a lack of clear definition in management's expectation of the personnel function, and a corresponding reticence among personnel managers to indicate what they felt this role should be. The authors of the report felt that the unclear definition of personnel responsibilities was the root of many of the problems found in the personnel department. This lack of definition applied to the purpose of the personnel function, the relationship of the personnel function to line management, and the relationship to other departments on personnel matters.

The findings also indicated that the personnel function is perceived by others as the administration of routine, maintenance, housekeeping tasks. It is seen as a department waiting to be consulted on personnel problems. Furthermore, it is perceived as:

1. Reacting to, rather than anticipating problems.
2. Passive — not an initiator nor a stimulator.
3. Defending the status quo rather than being creative and attempting to exercise leadership.
4. Carrying out management decisions, but not helping to shape management thinking.
5. Not standing up to be counted.
6. Not a risk-taker.
7. Not business-oriented.
8. Not involved in the personnel aspects of business decisions.
9. Having very little influence with management.
10. Operating in a vacuum.

Perceptions were also obtained about the personnel manager. He was viewed by others in the organization primarily as a consultant, counselor, and sounding board on personnel matters to his immediate supervisor and other managers. The personnel manager's rewards were viewed as coming primarily from consulting and, consequently, he had little time or desire to plan and innovate or to develop effective personnel systems. The personnel manager spent much time consulting with management which made the personnel function as a whole seem passive.

The study of the professional skills of personnel manpower disclosed three main problem areas: insufficient professionalism; overemphasis on the generalist; relative lack of skills, not only in the required fundamental, but also in innovative, research, and planning activities. On the matter of insufficient professionalism, the researchers found that the line managers in all functions took pride in their ability to handle people. This put the personnel manager at a disadvantage. He constantly had to relate to others who considered themselves experts on people and personnel matters. This view, consistently expressed, might be due to the fact that many people in personnel lacked the formal education and training in the related professional disciplines and/or the personal skills required to cope with this situation.

There was an overemphasis on the personnel generalist because in the organization such a type received the greatest rewards. Many people in specialized corporate personnel positions were actually generalists passing through briefly for development purposes. It was common for a division or plant generalist to have had more expertise than the corporate specialist. The researchers found a relative lack of skills in personnel. Few had successfully demonstrated abilities in manpower planning, career path planning, organization planning, personnel research, and intra- and intergroup conflict resolution. There is much to know about personnel and it is impossible for any one person to know it all, but the company gave insufficient recognition to the person specializing in a particular activity. Therefore, the personnel activity in general suffered and there were too few fully qualified specialists to whom the generalists could turn for help.

There was no clear understanding of the responsibilities and relationships within the personnel function. The expectations of corporate management were not clearly understood. This lack of understanding had the following results:

# THE PERSONNEL DEPARTMENT

1. Lack of integration, coordination of effort, and unity of purpose between provincial personnel units that perceived themselves to be self-sufficient.

2. Lack of adequate attention from personnel to such groups as the corporate functional departments, the division field sales organizations, and distribution centers.

3. Overlapping responsibility between personnel units.

4. Highly compartmentalized corporate personnel departments that should but did not operate on an open, fully coordinated basis.

The personnel function lacked sufficient capacity to work in such problem areas as minority group relations, the needs of younger workers, the needs of high talent personnel, and the like. Finally, in a variety of areas, the personnel department had yet to set up adequate functions to handle new and growing problems.

To resolve some of these problems, the task force made a series of recommendations which are extremely interesting from the view of this whole study. It felt that corporate management had not thoroughly defined what it expected of corporate and division personnel functions. It also found that personnel executives had not successfully assisted management in defining organization responsibilities and the required skills needed to perform personnel activities. It recommended, first, that personnel must establish clear guidelines and secure management's approval of personnel's role in relation to the company's needs. Within this framework, personnel must take the leadership in increasing corporate sensitivity to the environment and adaptability to required changes. Second, they felt that corporate management should make clear, and confirm by actual practice, who is the senior personnel officer of the company. In the third place, they felt that a more precise definition of the personnel role would lead to clear standards of professional skills. They felt that the organization should then upgrade personnel by (a) attracting more young professionals, and (b) providing more development opportunities for those currently employed.

Two general findings in the company report are most important in light of the national study: (1) lack of professionalism in personnel; (2) acceptance of what we have called the mythical image of the personnel manager as a compromiser and an advisor.

In order to gain further insight into the second conclusion, the company made available the verbatim notes on all the interviews. In the ensuing pages, the views of personnel from these five perspectives will be given: top level management; middle and division management;

plant management; top level personnel management; plant personnel management.

## Top level management

One top level manager had a generally negative view of the over-all personnel function. He did not believe that it provided much consulting service but performed strictly a maintenance function and did little, if any, advising. He felt that all he had to do was "touch base" with corporate personnel, but felt he must neutralize division management to prevent it from hindering him. This official would prefer that the personnel department do little and eventually become purely a research function.

Another manager felt that the personnel department had been weak, but foresaw a more important role for personnel in the future. In his view, personnel departments should be consulted and permitted to react on *all* matters. They should be put in a position to participate on all major corporate issues.

A third manager had a somewhat more positive view of the personnel function. He felt that only ten years ago personnel people were intimidated in the business environment but now were more confident, more independent, and impatient with a sluggish, slow-moving company. When this man worked at the division level he tried to involve personnel in all matters related to the human element of work.

Another top manager felt that personnel had had a negative image, but that it had gradually improved. However, he felt that personnel was still plagued by narrow thinking at both the divisional and corporate levels. Personnel administrators should have experience in other facets of the business so that they could get a broader view of their own function.

Still another manager felt that all personnel functions were never "forward-looking enough" for top management, and this had led top management to withhold its support of the function. Furthermore, the corporate personnel department had not had the "courage" to tell top management when it was wrong. The function needed to be more active and aggressive, to do more than react only when a problem had been raised by top management. Corporate personnel was hindered by the fact that top management felt it knew more about personnel matters than the personnel department. This is unlike management's attitude toward other departments (e.g. engineering, accounting) in which management knows it does not have the expertise of these staff departments. This was a basic problem for the personnel manager.

One top manager was struck by the increasing complexity of human problems. These require particular attention and, therefore, the personnel function has become stronger. This respondent had no idea that a man in his spot would be plagued with so many personnel problems. He felt personnel managers should carry more weight with the management by having the necessary expertise. He believed that personnel should not be just a service department designed to give management what it wanted. What was needed was leadership.

Another respondent had a number of relevant views about the personnel function. He believed it responded, instead of taking the lead, was highly routine, and was lacking in professionalism and conceptual theory. He rated personnel at the lower end of the occupational continuum, well below other staff departments such as law, purchasing, and engineering. Despite his glum assessment of the personnel function, he felt that the department should do more: "They should exert leadership at the corporate staff level. . . . should be pioneering changes in policy and personnel action." In conclusion, he contended that "they had better play a more important role in the future."

In sum, this highest level of corporate management was generally critical of the personnel function. It should be pointed out, however, that the study was designed to evoke mainly criticism. Most respondents seemed to feel that personnel had not been sufficiently aggressive and innovative in the past but that the personnel function had been improving and would continue to grow stronger in the future.

*Middle and division management (second-level management)*

The next group of respondents, also high level managers, were slightly lower in the management hierarchy.

The first middle-level manager felt that the personnel department was a good source of information, but was too easily cowed by top management. He viewed it as not business oriented, in need of a clearer definition of its role, and greater creativity. He also felt that top management was not clear on what were the personnel functions.

Another manager at this level was more impressed with personnel at the division level than at the corporate level. Nevertheless, even within his own division, he would not call on the personnel department unless the situation was extremely serious. He felt that he was as expert on personnel matters as his personnel people. "I guess I would have to say that I'm the top personnel manager in this division." He felt that the most important contribution his personnel manager could make was to keep him posted and give him feedback on his performances.

Still another viewed personnel as a conglomerate of more or less disjointed functions. However, he felt that its services were done in a reasonably professional manner. He would like to see personnel freed of its "trash-can" aspect. His area needed another personnel man to help handle the administrative workload so that the personnel manager's time could be freed for other important things. This manager conceded an important role to personnel, but still mainly advisory. He expected the division personnel manager to be a skilled counsellor to key managers, including himself. He regarded the personnel manager as influential and rated him along with line management in making decisions on personnel problems.

A fourth middle-level manager also had a positive view of the personnel functions: "The major role of the department should be acting as a listening post, which contributes to the awareness of the general manager to what is going on regarding people. He should act as a sounding board for major 'people type' problems." He felt personnel people should be decision-makers, although he claimed that currently they do not assume this role. Personnel must be more aggressive in this area and also place more emphasis on creativity. He believed that personnel should take the leadership in introducing, initiating, planning, and carrying through new programs. Also, personnel should be giving the corporation guidance on organizational changes. Nevertheless, he, too, regarded himself as the expert on personnel matters: "I feel that departments other than personnel have demonstrated more leadership. In part, this may be because I feel that I am something of a personnel expert myself, whereas I have to rely more on other departments."

The final middle-level manager interviewed saw the division personnel manager as being his alter ego in managing personnel. That is, he did his thinking for him in regard to people. The personnel manager kept the division out of trouble when it came to personnel issues. This middle-level manager's views of corporate personnel were more negative. In general, he felt that personnel could improve and make a greater contribution by taking a more aggressive position. He expected the personnel department to come up with ideas, suggestions, or recommendations — not merely react to the ideas of others.

These second-level managers dealt more with personnel at the division level and, in general, were more satisfied with their performance. They gave personnel a greater role today and saw them performing even more centrally in the future.

In the next section, the descent down the management hierarchy is to the plant management level. These managers are found taking an even stronger positive view of the personnel function.

## Plant management

One plant manager felt that the plant personnel department had been not only very helpful but also had influenced and contributed to plant decisions. (For the first time, we find a reference to a personnel man as a decision-maker.)

Another plant manager felt that his plant personnel department was still seeking its niche. However, he did consult with them on problems of minority groups and the role of the foreman. He expected them to keep peace with the union.

Still another felt that, since the company's primary orientation was marketing, personnel had relatively low status. However, in his view, all levels of the personnel function had been helpful in labor relations, recruiting, benefits, and hiring.

The last plant manager interviewed believed it unfortunate that personnel played such a minor role in the operation of the plant. He discussed all personnel decisions with the personnel manager. The plant personnel manager was always available to him for advice and consultation, and had been particularly effective as a sounding board. He felt the plant personnel manager had helped him in innumerable ways. In his view, personnel was directly involved in the management of the plant. He did not know of any areas in which personnel might make greater contributions. It had marked influence on all areas dealing with personnel matters. Over-all, he felt that the personnel group had a relatively strong impact on the entire business.

The clearest conclusion drawn from the views of management is that personnel is viewed as a much more potent force at the plant level than at the division or corporate levels. Opinions of personnel declined markedly with ascent of the management hierarchy. The explanation of this does much to reconcile previous findings about independent action with the prevailing occupational myth. More independent behavior at the plant level may be explained by the probability that the younger men there have been more exposed to the "professional" view of personnel administration. Consequently, their behavior is viewed as more professional, more independent, and more innovative. On the other hand, personnel officers at the division and corporate levels are probably older and more likely to have the trash-can and/or welfare view of personnel — hence, their relative impotence.

On further analysis, it is observed that criticisms by top management of corporate and division personnel managers were, in the main, quite general. They castigated them for "lack of initiative," "little creativity," "narrow thinking," and not being "forward-looking." Plant managers, on the contrary, commented on plant personnel managers in more concrete terms. They praised or criticized them for their work on certain specifics. It may be that top management is criticizing, more than anything else, their image of personnel and the mythical image that personnel tries to project. Whereas, the plant managers may not be concerned with real or imaginary images but rather with actual performance.

The following example illustrates that point. A top corporate personnel officer claimed that he never made any decisions. However, when specific instances were discussed it was clear that he did, in fact, make decisions. His method made it appear as if top management had made them. It was this same personnel executive who decided that this case study should be undertaken. He first discreetly convinced top management of the need for such a study. Several months after initiating his discussions with top management, it was apparently "suddenly decided" by the management to do a study of the personnel function. This kind of "undercover decision-making" perpetuates the myth that personnel men are nondecision-makers.

*Top level personnel management*

In general, the top level personnel managers were more concerned with personnel as it should be than with personnel as it actually is.

One man in this group felt that the role of personnel was to recruit, place, and utilize effectively the human resources of the corporation consistent with over-all business objectives. He felt that personnel must convince top management that they are professionals and experts on human matters. Personnel must "act, instead of react," not be "a happiness boy," and be more oriented toward the behavioral sciences. In addition, personnel must become increasingly active in major social issues in both the company and the community. He felt that corporate personnel had the authority to get the job done — however, "we have more authority than we exercise." He deplored the fact that personnel had not been involved in high level job placement, promotions, and even important labor relations matters. Personnel must become active in these functions and assume the "responsibility for introducing new ideas."

Another top level personnel manager generally concurred with the above view. He saw personnel as having line responsibility in such areas as employment, but acting only as advisors and consultants on other important issues. Top management had actively kept personnel out of areas such as negotiations. He believed that top management would like to have corporate personnel play a more active role in negotiations, but politically they could not allow it; they would lose points if they gave up these functions. This personnel man recognized that he had, even now, a good deal of influence. He felt he had influence on operating decisions if only as a consultant. "I feel I can get things done, but basically have responsibility without any authority." "Many times I would like to issue edicts...." "I feel free to speak my mind."

A third top level personnel manager saw personnel as changing and "for the first time setting up long-range plans within the area...." "We must become a planner rather than an actor." Despite these changes, he "is frustrated by the amount of authority he has to get personnel things done in the company."

Still another reflected the split between occupational image and reality. On the other hand, he said, he had no influence outside his own area, but he also said that he got total acceptance by the president on a number of recommendations made by his department. In addition, he felt certain that his suggestions were accepted by the operating people.

The next top level personnel manager felt that personnel should "be a change agent, and have the courage to stand up and be counted." Still another felt that his "role has grown more significant in the last five years." A final corporate personnel manager saw "personnel moving toward a position where they have weight and are not just a hand holder."

Over-all, it appeared that corporate personnel managers viewed the personnel function as improving and moving in the direction of greater stature.

## Plant personnel management

The first plant personnel manager felt that plant personnel people had more influence on plant operators than the corporate personnel vice-president had on corporate operations. This was because results could be achieved faster in the plant than at headquarters. Quicker results may be part of the reason for the greater influence of the personnel function at the plant level.

Another also felt that "in the field locations personnel is more involved with business than at the corporate level." "Personnel departments in the plant are much stronger." He felt that he played a strong role in making a contribution to the company.

One other felt that "personnel is too much of a service organization and a catch-all function." "It does not do enough planning, organizing, controlling."

The last one interviewed was highly critical of personnel at the plant level. He viewed it strictly as a service function and saw personnel as the lowest level staff department. He felt that the personnel function lacked enough authority to initiate any action. The personnel man was at the mercy of the line manager, in his view, because the personnel department showed no profit.

Plant personnel managers, for the most part, seemed to be more satisfied with their role and importance in the organization than were top level personnel managers. This parallels the conclusions of line managers. However, all expressed some dissatisfaction and desired more authority and power within the organization.

Upon analysis, the crux of the issue emerges as decision-making. Both this study of a single company and the nationwide survey clearly show that personnel administrators *do,* in fact, make decisions, but they *do not* have the authority to carry out their decisions. Lack of authority apparently had been confused with lack of decision-making ability. Even in the area of authority, however, many people, both in and out of personnel, recognize that personnel is moving in the direction of greater status.

Personnel men do make decisions and these decisions are now made by those in the occupation who are more professional than their predecessors. Once personnel people and top management recognize the personnel administrator as a decision-maker, then authority to carry out decisions will follow. What is needed is an effort by all to overcome the mythical images of the personnel department and deal with what actually takes place.

# THE PERSONNEL DEPARTMENT

In all fairness it should be noted that a personnel executive of the company in this study did not concur with the conclusions about the personnel manager as a decision-maker. The following is his opinion:

> The personnel managers are key members of the group involved in making personnel decisions. Most decisions made in an organization such as an industrial firm are the result of discussion among a number of people, frequently from different functions. (The decision itself may be considered a compromise, consensus, etc.) It is difficult to pinpoint any one person as being solely responsible for a decision.
>
> The role of the personnel function on decisions regarding personnel matters is fourfold:
>
> - to affect agreement from management as to the systems and processes that should serve as the context within which personnel decisions are made;
> - to administer and monitor these systems and processes;
> - to provide expert opinion in the development and administration of these systems and processes; and, finally,
> - to participate as one of the group involved in making a personnel decision.

We do not believe that we are in basic disagreement with the views of this personnel administrator. We do not claim that the personnel manager is "solely responsible" for decisions. We seek only to demonstrate that personnel administrators *do* make decisions and on this the above personnel administrator seems to agree.

# CHAPTER 8

# Conclusions

ONE major problem in the sociological study of occupations, already mentioned in Chapter 1, is that it has mainly been composed of descriptive studies. Everett Hughes provided most of the impetus for the study of occupations and his orientation was virtually atheoretical. He presented his rationale for studying occupations as follows:

> It is of importance for the understanding of human work—in the industrial and in other settings—that we develop a set of problems and processes applicable to the whole range of cases. The terms for describing these problems and processes can be got by comparison of the work drama in various occupations....In so studying work, we are not merely applying sociology to work. We are studying work by sociological methods....We may learn about society by studying industry and human work generally. In our particular society, work organization looms so large as a separate and specialized system of things, and work experience is so fateful a part of every man's life, that we cannot make much headway as students of society and of social psychology without using work as one of our main laboratories.[1]

For Hughes and for his students the study of work was important because: (a) by studying particular occupations one can determine "problems and processes" applicable to all occupations; and (b) by studying occupations one can learn about society.

[1]Everett Hughes, "The Sociological Study of Work: An Editorial Foreword," *American Journal of Sociology*, vol. 57, no. 5 (March 1952), p. 426.

## CONCLUSIONS

Although these points are undoubtedly valid, they leave the sociologist without any theoretical tools with which to analyze occupations. Consequently, the field of occupational sociology has been dominated by purely observational studies of a series of occupations. These offer insight into social and occupational structure, but they have yet to be codified.

In this book's chapter, "Behavior in Role Conflict Situations," an attempt was made to apply some of the concepts of role theory to the study of the personnel manager. It is believed that role theory offers the occupational sociologist the tools to analyze occupations. When one examines the studies of particular occupations it becomes clear that role concepts are at least implicit in the analyses. Concepts such as role, position, role set, role conflict, and role ambiguity are applicable and useful in each of these studies. In the present study of the personnel officer, role theory was explicitly employed. As a matter of fact, part of the study was designed to retest some aspects of Gross, Mason, and McEachern's theory of role conflict resolution and to determine whether certain relevant points were omitted from their study.[2] Although the goal was theoretical, there is no reason why role theory could not be employed equally well in descriptive studies of particular occupations.

In terms of the Gross, Mason, and McEachern study, the following are salient findings of the present study:

1. The modes of resolution of role conflict posited by Gross, *et al.* — conforming to the expectations of the most powerful of two significant others when they were in conflict, and compromise — were confirmed as viable means of resolving role conflict.

2. Some doubt was cast upon withdrawal as a realistic means of resolving role conflict, at least for personnel managers.

3. The preeminent mode of resolution is independent action, an alternative not considered in the Gross, Mason, and McEachern scheme. In all twelve situations studied, independent action was the most common choice; in eleven of the twelve situations, it was chosen significantly more often than the next most frequently chosen alternative.

4. The nature of the issue makes a difference in terms of how role conflict is resolved. Two different cases were used and the frequency of choice for the behavioral alternatives varied from one case to the

[2]Neal Gross, Ward S. Mason, and Alexander W. McEachern, *Explorations in Role Analysis* (New York: John Wiley, 1958).

other. For example, there was greater likelihood to resolve conflict in favor of the accounting manager in Case 1 because that case involved a monetary issue. In Case 2, where no money was involved, the power of the accounting manager declined as did resolutions in his favor.

5. When confronted with a powerful and weak significant other, the focal role is likely to resolve in the direction of the more powerful one.

6. When the focal role is confronted with only powerful significant others, he is more likely to compromise.

7. When the focal role is confronted with two weak significant others, he is more likely to take independent action.

The important theoretical contribution here on professionalism relates to the fact that the literature so far has failed to differentiate between the occupational and individual levels of professionalism. Most of it has been concerned only with the occupational level — that is, it has sought to determine what differentiates a professional occupation from the less professional or nonprofessional occupations. An equally important question is what differentiates a professional individual from a less or nonprofessional individual. Thus, it is possible to have a nonprofessonal doctor even in the highly professional medical profession. On the other hand, it is also conceivable to have a professional janitor in the nonprofessional janitorial occupation. What needs to be determined is what attitudinal and experiential variables differentiate between professional and nonprofessional individuals.

On the occupational level, the Wilensky stage[3] approach and a structural functional approach were used to determine the degree of professionalism of the personnel occupations.[4] Both techniques, one historical and the other ahistorical, indicate that the personnel occupations have some professional characteristics, but are lacking on a number of others.

On the individual level, the picture is essentially the same. Although there are some individuals with professional characteristics, the majority seem to be lacking in them.

In Chapter 4, an effort was made to determine the commitment of personnel managers to their organization and occupation by retesting

[3]Harold Wilensky, "The Professionalization of Everyone?" *AJS*, vol. 70, no. 2 (September 1964), pp. 137–158.

[4]Robert Habenstein, "Critique of 'Profession' as a Sociological Category," *Sociological Quarterly*, vol. 4, no. 4, 1963, pp. 294–297.

# CONCLUSIONS

Howard Becker's side-bet theory.[5] Over-all, personnel managers are slightly more committed to their occupations than to their employing organization. Furthermore, the data indicate that side bets do not account for commitment to organization. An alternative theory of commitment contends that organizational commitment is a residual category. One first attempts to commit himself to his occupation. How committed he becomes is determined by the meaningfulness of that occupation. If the occupation has meaningless or trivial aspects, the individual supplements occupational commitment with organizational commitment in order to make his work life meaningful. Since the personnel occupation is only partially meaningful, the personnel manager supplements his moderate occupational commitment with some commitment to his organization.

Each of the theoretical foci has generated data which reveal much about the nature of the personnel occupations. Demographically and behaviorally, a number of findings bear repeating:

1. Personnel managers as well as members of the two other personnel occupations studied (employment managers and vice-presidents) are highly educated. This seems to reflect the claim of increasing professionalism of the personnel occupations. It confirms an historical change in personnel administration. Personnel people are no longer simply rejects from line management, but are highly trained specialists in personnel matters. This is affirmed by the fact that 60 percent of each group majored in personnel or the related fields of behavioral science or business administration.

2. All three groups of personnel administrators exhibited a high degree of intergenerational mobility both at the occupational and educational level. In the main, personnel administrators have come from fairly modest backgrounds and have been able to far outstrip their fathers.

3. There is some evidence that vice-presidents of personnel come from somewhat different family backgrounds than persons in the other two occupations. This may indicate there is no career pattern of progression from employment manager to vice-president of personnel. Only those from certain backgrounds generally qualify for the position of vice-president. This is supported by the fact that, while 92 percent of vice-presidents had been personnel managers, only 24 percent had, at any time in their careers, been employment managers.

[5]Howard Becker, "Notes on the Concept of Commitment," *American Journal of Sociology*, vol. 66, 1960, pp. 32–42.

4. On activities performed by personnel managers, the only surprising finding is the relatively large percentage of time (13 percent) spent on making decisions for other departments in the company. This is in line with the finding that personnel managers are, in fact, decision-makers.

5. Personnel managers feel that they should be spending more time on planning personnel department activities, representing the company in outside organizations, providing information and advice for decision-making by others, and involving themselves in professional functions. On the other hand, they feel they should be spending less time supervising subordinates, representing the company to the union, gathering information, and making decisions on personnel matters for other departments in the company. The latter finding is surprising in the face of our data which indicate that personnel managers are decision-makers. However, it is explicable in the sense that it represents support for the mythical image of the personnel manager as a non-decision-maker. When asked what they do, personnel managers indicate that they make decisions; but when asked what they should do, they feel they should do less decision-making. An interpretation of this paradox is that the "should" probably represents a continuing subscription to the occupational myth which their self-reported actions contradict.

Professionally lacking on both the individual and occupational levels, personnel must take action at both levels if it wishes to become professional. Before suggesting steps which might be taken, this question must be answered: *Does personnel administration want to become more professional?*

In a foreword to an article by the authors in *The Personnel Administrator,* the president of the American Society for Personnel Administration has this to say:

> Inevitably, we have to come to grips with the matter of professionalism in personnel. As we learn more, a new concept is beginning to emerge. It is becoming increasingly clear to some of us that ASPA and Cornell may make a unique pioneering type contribution by defining a new set of criteria for the professionalization of functions which operate within the framework of an established organization.

> Those of us who believe strongly that the practicing personnel man must be completely involved and immersed in the day-to-day operations of the enterprise if he is to properly focus "manpower management" as a key element in the success of the organization,

would be reluctant to espouse a concept of professionalism which would tend to isolate the function from business reality.

Thus, while we may borrow from the criteria utilized by such established groups as medicine, law and teaching to determine what constitutes professionalism, we may also modify and add. Perhaps we will produce a model which will better serve those functions which, like personnel, demand and are willing to earn a better defined role in our rapidly changing society.[6]

It is clearly a moot point as to whether or not personnel really wants to become professional in the traditional sense. So far, a professional model applicable to it is lacking; without it, only some practical suggestions based on the traditional professional model can be made:

*Occupational level*

1. An effort should be made to unify the numerous professional personnel associations into one cohesive body.

2. Once a central national body is formed, certification could be a feasible second objective.

3. A code of ethics needs to be set forth by the national body; one which would have an impact on personnel administrators.

4. Effort is needed to define clearly what body of knowledge is the exclusive domain of personnel administrators.

5. Organization executives and the public must be educated to recognize the particular expertise of personnel administrators and their ability to handle "people problems."

6. Personnel administrators need to define their function and who their clients are.

7. Personnel administrators must recognize that they are independent decision-makers and authority-wielders.

*Individual level*

1. Efforts must be made to insure that those who enter personnel in the future are well educated and have majored in personnel or related fields.

2. Public relations is needed at the college level to make personnel a more attractive vocation. This would lead to more people majoring, while in school, in personnel administration.

[6]Robert L. Berra, foreword to George Ritzer, Harrison Trice, and Susan Gottesmann, "Profile of a Professional," *The Personnel Administrator,* vol. 13, no. 6 (November–December 1968), p. 1.

3. Increased use of the sponsorship pattern can help to inculcate neophyte personnel administrators with professional values.

4. The professional association must encourage greater activity by the members in the association.

These are some things personnel can do to become more professional. Those concerned alone can answer whether or not they *want* to become professional.

The material on commitment indicates that personnel managers are committed to both occupation and organization. It may well be that such dual commitment is a source of dissatisfaction and anxiety to personnel managers. This issue will probably be resolved if personnel managers decide to become professional. Occupational commitment will then increase, while organizational commitment will decline. If, on the other hand, personnel does not professionalize, it will continue the dual commitment, an uncomfortable but not unbearable situation.

Especially important to personnel is the finding that personnel managers are independent decision-makers. This stands in contradiction to the generally held concept that they are compromisers, and passive nondecision-makers. This image is substantiated by a variety of sources. In a recent article the following phrases were used to describe the personnel officer: "glorified clerks," "they have no backbone and always find some way to accommodate the wishes of the strongest forces acting on them," "the personnel officer is traditionally non-activist, not a positive force," "he (the personnel officer) isn't sufficiently assertive."[7]

Even in Strauss and Sayles' popular textbook this image is fostered: "Perhaps the most common behavior pattern of all, or at least the one most often associated with personnel managers, is serving as an advisor....The personnel man on request supplies technical information, counsel, and recommendations to assist another manager in making a decision or solving a problem."[8] They go on to say that there are areas in which personnel managers make decisions (e.g. merit raises), but they come to the following conclusion: "Although personnel managers have technical expertise in activities of this sort, it is our view that they should not be permitted to establish the organization's criteria for supervisory success. All the policies, objectives, and

[7]O. Glenn Stahl, "Tomorrow's Generation of Personnel Managers," paper presented at the Public Personnel Association, International Conference, Victoria, B. C., October 1967.

[8]George Strauss and Leonard Sayles, *Personnel,* 2nd ed. (Englewood Cliffs, N. J.: Prentice-Hall, 1967), p. 431.

standards of the company are so integrally related to one another that line management — line management alone — must retain the responsibility for determining them. The staff can provide information from which the line can base its decisions, of course...that line management should decide...."[9]

The surprising thing about this image is that most people recognize it as a myth. Strauss and Sayles have some strong support for this point. Their list of the "elements that seem to characterize a healthy advisor relationship" clearly indicates that under the guise of being advisors, personnel managers are making the decisions for, or manipulating the decisions of, line management. Only one of their list of elements is here quoted to illustrate the point: "Personnel staff develops greater acceptance for its ideas and points of view, not through putting pressure on the line supervisor to 'change or else,' but through developing confidence in the staff's helping role through proving in practice that it can contribute to the supervisor's effectiveness."[10]

An even bolder description of the personnel manager as a manipulative decision-maker appears in the following statement by a personnel officer:

> We can't tell the managers or the foreman what to do. Of course we do set the policies and they have to follow them. We could make a big fuss if they don't follow policies, but usually we don't have to. As a matter of fact, they are in on the policy decisions in the first place, and usually we can get them to understand the reasons why they must act as we have planned....When the guys in the line don't want to follow a certain policy or practice, we usually think there is probably a reason for it. Then we try to find out what that reason is, so we can help them. We know that there is more than one way to skin a cat, so we find out what they want to do; we find a legitimate way to get the cat skinned.[11]

The personnel manager is very often not as subtle as these descriptions would lead one to believe. The following anecdote from a study by Dalton McFarland illustrates a more authoritarian type of personnel manager:

> The personnel director had recently tried to persuade the plant man to follow his ideas about paying employees' moving expenses when

[9]*ibid.*, p. 435.
[10]*ibid.*, p. 434.
[11]Dalton McFarland, *Cooperation and Conflict in Personnel Administration*, (New York: American Foundation for Management Research, 1962), p. 126.

*83*

there was a relocation. The president assured him that plant mana-gers are in complete charge and that corporate staff people only advise and counsel. The plant manager answered: "Well, it doesn't seem that way to me!" The answer of the company president was perhaps a classic capsule statement of an attitude toward line-staff conflict: "Of course you feel that way, and I think you should feel that way. I want the personnel director to be so persuasive and so effective that it will bother you a little when you ignore his advice!"[12]

The findings in this study, and the existence of the mythical image of the personnel director as a compromiser, are both explainable in terms of the nature of the personnel occupations. The propensity toward independent action reflects the current trend toward profes-sionalization among personnel managers. By taking independent action in role conflict situations, they are exhibiting the professional charac-teristic of autonomy. The fact that the compromise choice is the second most popular probably reflects the lingering welfare and trash-can ideologies. It is even possible for a personnel manager to be both a compromiser and to take independent action in different situations. These individuals reflect the *dual orientation* in the occupation.

Why do personnel managers claim that they are not decision-makers, when the evidence from the present study and other sources clearly indicates that they often make independent decisions? The answer in part is that the nondecision-maker myth is a carry-over from the early years of personnel. As the occupation has become more impor-tant, its shift from trivial work and mere advising has not been fully recognized either by personnel or by others in the organization.

This myth seems to be functional for the personnel manager. Although he claims no authority over a line manager, he does in fact give him orders under the guise of advice. Both the personnel manager and the line manager know that the advice is thinly veiled command. They are content, however, to have it appear as advice upon which the line manager makes the decision. This charade abets and continues the myth.

The functionality of this occupational myth aids the personnel manager in maintaining precarious organizational relationships. Deal-ing with the notion on a more general level, Dubin takes essentially the same position: "Organizational fictions are those fictions that are necessary in order that action within the formal organization may

12*ibid.*, p. 3.

proceed."[13] By allowing the significant others to believe that they make the decisions, the personnel manager maintains his power. If it was made explicit, there would probably be line managers who would drastically change their attitude toward the personnel department. Taking orders from a staff man, especially a personnel manager, is opposed to every myth the line manager has ever learned. In order to retain the precarious status quo, both parties continue the charade. Once again, Dubin takes a similar position: "The truth, however, is disconcerting so by a kind of salient agreement among members of the organization, this truth is clothed in a fiction."[14]

Finally, since too often studies of occupations have been without a theoretical focus, this application of occupational sociology to the personnel occupations offers a sample of what can be done. The personnel occupations, by virtue of their position in the organization, offer a fertile field for the inquiring occupational sociologist. By focusing on such central sociological questions as conflict resolution, commitment, and professionalism, this study has highlighted some heretofore ignored problems for the practicing administrator. The data reported can now be used to understand his occupational position better. Above all, this study points up the need to relate sociological findings to the practical problems confronting specific occupations. Occupational sociology cannot be divorced from reality and, conversely, the study of occupations should not be divorced from theory.

[13]Dubin, p. 341.
[14]*ibid.*, p. 343.

# APPENDIX A

# Methodology: Evolution of the Questionnaire

This study of the personnel function employed a nationwide, anonymous questionnaire and a series of in-depth interviews. The format for the questionnaire was completed in June 1967. Over the next several months eighty interviews were held to pretest the questionnaire. As a result of these interviews, several changes were made. A mail pretest was begun on September 6, 1967, handled by the American Society for Personnel Administration from its headquarters in Berea, Ohio.

Questionnaires were mailed to a systematic, stratified sample of 117 members of ASPA, including 96 personnel managers. Of the 2,410 personnel managers on whom this study largely concentrated, every twenty-fifth name was drawn from the alphabetical listing. Two weeks after the initial mailing, a reminder letter was sent. The response rate from these two mailings was just over 50 percent (59 out of 117). This was promising, especially since the questionnaire was sixteen pages long. However, more effort was needed to obtain the higher response rate desired for the final study.

A comment sheet was included with the pretest questionnaire. The elicited comments indicated that still more changes were required to perfect the questionnaire. These changes were made and pretested on 30 more personnel managers. This last pretest resulted in a few additional changes. No further pretesting was deemed necessary because the changes made were of such a minor nature.

The first half of the questionnaire contained questions on demographic variables, work history, commitment to the organization, commitment to the occupation, degree of perceived role conflict, and a short form of the authoritarianism scale (finally not used). This part of the questionnaire was routine and need not be discussed here. The bulk of the questionnaire was devoted to two conflict situations and the evolution of this part of the questionnaire will be detailed.

In the first questionnaire mailed, the respondent was asked to write a paragraph describing a conflict situation he had recently faced. The respondent was then asked to write a second paragraph describing the actions taken to resolve this conflict. Too many problems arose in coding and analyzing this kind of data. Also, since so much writing was required of respondents, it was decided that this approach probably would result in a low response rate.

The decision to discard the open-ended method left the problem of how to devise a closed-ended series of questions aimed at studying respondents' approaches to conflict resolution. This basic approach was decided upon: a series of realistic cases were to be described in detail; key significant others who might be involved in such cases were listed; one significant other would advise taking one action while another would advise exactly the opposite; in this way each significant figure was paired with all of the other key figures. After each of these pairings, the respondent would be given a series of behavioral choices and was asked to choose his most likely action from them. Then he would rate each of the key figures on a series of variables (e.g. power, affect), critical in determining how the respondent said he would behave in each situation. This approach, despite minor alterations, remained the basic methodological device of the study.

It is pertinent to describe how the hypothetical situations were obtained. An early decision was that general situations would not be useful because "real life" conflict resolution occurs in very specific situations. By restricting the cases to real situations, it was felt that the incidence of general, stereotyped responses could be greatly reduced. What was necessary was a number of cases which are common to most, if not all, personnel managers. The literature on personnel administration proved to be a blind alley, since it dealt with personnel problems in very general terms. However, a series of interviews that students in Professor Harrison Trice's course in Personnel Administration at Cornell University had conducted with personnel managers contained detailed descriptions of typical situations. The first cases were drawn from this material. However, they were greatly altered as a result of the series of pretests which followed.

## Initial pretests

The first attempt at studying conflict resolution was presented as follows:

> Your immediate superior is in favor of hiring applicant A, but the plant manager is in favor of hiring applicant B.
>
> Not applicable_____
>
> _____A)  Hire applicant A
> _____B)  Hire applicant B
> _____C)  Attempt to reconcile conflicting demands
> _____D)  Refuse to listen to both your immediate superior and the plant manager and make it clear to them that you will make your own decision
> _____E)  Quit your job because you cannot work under such conflicting pressure
> _____F)  Do nothing
> _____G)  _____

In this initial version there were 21 such situations. They involved the pairing of each of the following significant figures with every other one: immediate superior, plant manager, immediate subordinate, plant production manager, foreman of the department for which the applicant is being hired, local union president, company president. An example of a different pairing in the same situation would be: Your immediate subordinate is in favor of hiring applicant A, but the plant production manager is in favor of hiring applicant B. After each pairing the respondent was given the same behavioral alternatives as in the first example. The seven behavioral alternatives given after each pairing represented expansion of a scheme developed by Gross, Mason, and MacEachern.[1] Alternatives A, B, C, and E were the four used by them. Choice D represented the hypothesis that an independent course of action is a viable alternative in such situations. The information on hand about personnel managers indicated that F, "do nothing," was also a possible choice. In order to be sure that all possible alternatives were covered, the blank choice G was included.

After considering the 21 pairings, the respondent was asked to rate each of the seven significant others on three variables: power, legitimacy, and the amount of visibility each had of the focal role. Power and legitimacy are the two role variables considered critical by Gross, Mason, and MacEachern. Alutto[2] (1967) suggested visibility as a third important variable. The following question on legitimacy exemplifies the questions asked about power and visibility:

> Please rate the following positions, on the basis of your past experience with them on the issue of hiring, in terms of how legitimate you feel it is for them to expect you to follow their advice on which of the applicants we have described to hire. (Where you have no contact with one of the positions listed, on this issue, do not rate that position.)
>
> a–Your immediate superior—(no legit.) 1 2 3 4 5 6 7 (much legit.)
> b–Your immediate subordinate—(no legit.) 1 2 3 4 5 6 7 (much legit.)
> c–Plant manager—(no legit.) 1 2 3 4 5 6 7 (much legit.)
> d–Plant production manager—(no legit.) 1 2 3 4 5 6 7 (much legit.)
> e–Department foreman—(no legit.) 1 2 3 4 5 6 7 (much legit.)
> f–Local union president—(no legit.) 1 2 3 4 5 6 7 (much legit.)
> g–Company president—(no legit.) 1 2 3 4 5 6 7 (much legit.)

With this preliminary approach in hand, a number of personnel managers and professors of personnel administration were asked for their evaluations. Several inadequacies were revealed by them. For instance, they thought more information about the case was required, and precise instructions on how to answer the questions were needed. Also, it was felt that there were too many

[1]Neal Gross, Ward Mason, and Alexander McEachern *Explorations in Role Analysis* (New York: John Wiley, 1958).

[2]Joseph Alutto, "Role Theory in Propositional Form," Ph.D. Dissertation, New York State School of Industrial and Labor Relations, Cornell University, 1967, pp. 42–44.

situations, and that by reducing the number of significant others the number of cases could be reduced.

Following these criticisms, the introduction and case information were expanded, thus:

> In this section we will pose a hypothetical situation and ask you to make a series of ratings and behavioral judgments. We would like you to try to make your ratings and judgments as if this was a real situation confronting you in your job. The situation is as follows: Several weeks ago you interviewed two applicants for a clerical position. You found both to be equally well qualified for the job. Yesterday an order came across your desk to hire a clerk. The decision on which clerk to hire has been left up to you, although it has been made clear that you cannot hire both.

The number of significant others involved was reduced from seven to five. The two eliminated were the company president and the plant production manager, the former as being too distant to be significant in this kind of case and the latter as having little to do with a hiring situation. The number of situations was reduced to ten. The respondent was asked to rate the five significant others on the same three role variables (power, legitimacy, and visibility). After each pairing, he was asked to make behavioral choices as before.

The questionnaire was then taken to New York City for a series of thirty pretest interviews with personnel managers. After only ten of these, it became clear that major revisions were again required. The ratings of the significant others on the three role variables, which had preceded the ten choice situations, were moved so that they followed the choices of behavioral alternatives. The pretests indicated that when the ratings came first, they tended to affect the choices made in the following situations. The case itself was changed because it was discovered that personnel managers are not often involved in hiring situations. The new case, as suggested by several personnel managers, read:

> Several weeks ago a terrible storm hit your area. Because of the storm most of your employees were unable to get to work. It is now your decision on whether to pay them for time lost due to the storm or not.

The significant persons involved were altered. The plant manager was eliminated because many respondents were in nonmanufacturing organizations. The foreman, also a manufacturing position, was changed to supervisor of one of the departments involved. The local union president was eliminated because many organizations were not unionized. As replacements, two new positions were added: the manager of the accounting department, and the top company official at the respondent's location.

After these changes were made, the remaining twenty pretests in New York were conducted. Once again, a number of revisions were called for. The case information was expanded in order to clarify certain points. It then read:

> Several weeks ago a terrible storm hit your area. Because of the storm a number of employees at your location were unable to get to work. The

employees involved were not in a union. This is the first time such a situation has occurred at your location and there is no policy or precedent on handling such an issue. You have thought over the situation and decided that there are good arguments for both paying and not paying the employees for the time lost. Although you are now neutral, you have been told that you must make a decision and that your decision will determine what the company will do. Since you are neutral, your decision will be based on what advice you receive from significant figures in your organization.

In order to reduce the number of choice situations following the case to six, one more of the significant others was eliminated; namely, the supervisor of one of the departments involved. "Your immediate superior" was changed to "the man immediately above you in the personnel department" because the former title did not indicate whether his superior in personnel or his line superior was intended. One of the behavioral choices was changed because it proved to be unrealistic. The original wording was, "Quit your job because you cannot work under such conflicting pressure." This option was never chosen in the pretest because it was too radical an action given the problem involved. The new wording still conveyed the basic idea of withdrawal. It read: "Withdraw from making a decision because you cannot work under such conflicting pressure." One other change resulting from this group of pretest interviews was addition of a fourth role variable which, the respondents believed, significantly affected decisions made in conflict situations. Expertise, the amount of knowledge each of the involved persons has of this type of problem, was added to legitimacy, power, and visibility. As before, the respondents were asked to rate the significant others on these variables.

At this point in the study, July 1967, several new research questions crystallized. An interest developed in whether or not people were consistent in their mode of resolving conflict. To answer this question, a second case in the same format was added. In addition, the respondent's previous experience with the type of situation and its importance to him were variables which it was felt should be brought out. Two questions were added, following the description of the case, asking for the respondent's evaluation of the case's relevance to him.

Following these changes further pretests were needed. Once again, twenty personnel managers in the metropolitan New York area suggested major alterations in the instrument. The "do nothing" behavioral choice was dropped because it was not a realistic alternative given their instructions to make a recommendation and, in fact, had never been chosen in over fifty pretests. Also, the blank choice, on the few occasions it was used, was easily assimilated by one of the five remaining coded choices. Removal of these two choices significantly reduced the length and complexity of the questionnaire.

In another major change, a fifth role variable was added. The pretests indicated that affect, or friendliness, was an important factor in determining how people resolved role conflict. Along with this, another change in the role variable section was made. It was found that *rating* the four significant figures from one to seven on the five role variables was an arduous task. The pretests indicated that *ranking* each of the figures in relation to each other on the five variables would greatly simplify the instrument and reduce the possibility of response set. In addition, several personnel managers complained that it was difficult to make fine distinctions when the rating system was used. The resistance to the rating was so great that it was decided to change to rankings, despite the fact that there would be some decline in the quality of the information obtained.

The wording for the behavioral alternative of compromise action was changed. It originally read: "Bring the two parties together and attempt to resolve their differences." Several respondents suggested that, although they might try to resolve differences, it would be extremely unlikely for them to bring certain parties (e.g. the top company official and their immediate superior) together. Responding to this valid criticism the wording was changed to: "Talk to the two parties and attempt to resolve their differences." The wording on the independent course of action was changed from "Listen to both, but make it clear to them that you will make your own decision" to "Listen to both, but make your own decision." The new wording was more parsimonious, but still conveyed essentially the same meaning. More problems were found with the behavioral alternative of withdrawal. On only two occasions in the pretest was "Withdraw from making a decision because you cannot work under such conflicting pressure" chosen. Several respondents indicated that its wording did not make it a viable alternative. The wording was changed to reflect withdrawal, but in a more realistic way. The new choice read: "Hold your recommendation in abeyance."

Changes of this magnitude necessitated, once again, further pretesting. The new questionnaire was administered to the members of a large, upstate New York personnel organization at one of its monthly meetings. It was also sent to other personnel managers who were asked to respond by mail. Over thirty responses were obtained from these two sources and two new suggestions were made and incorporated into the questionnaire. A question was added to each case to determine whether the respondent actually had contact with the other key persons listed. It was felt that respondents might deal quite differently with actual persons in their own organizations than they would with hypothetical people. The other change was designed to guard against response set in the behavioral choices. To prevent this, the five behavioral alternatives which followed each pairing of significant others were rotated after each choice situation. With these two changes the questionnaire had evolved into its final form. The final version of the questionnaire appears as Appendix B.

*Sample for final study*

All the personnel managers who had participated in any of the pretests and all female personnel managers were eliminated from the total ASPA membership lists. There remained 2,031 male personnel managers from which to choose a sample for final study. A 33 percent sample was decided upon, broken down by geographic regions since it was felt that this might be a significant variable affecting role conflict resolutions. Thus, a total of 677 personnel managers were sampled.

Fifty-four members of the sample could not be located, probably due to insufficient address or recently changed job. These might have been replaced but the information was not divulged by ASPA (which handled the mailing) until about two months after the study was in progress. The loss of fifty-four respondents was not considered crippling; it left a sample of 623 personnel managers.

The mailing, handled by ASPA headquarters in Berea, Ohio, began on November 27, 1967 and ended on December 5, 1967. A cover letter was signed by the president of ASPA because it was felt that his signature would be most influential. A reminder letter was sent on December 18, 1967.

By January 19, 1968 over 40 percent of the sample questionnaires had been completed and returned. On that day, all respondents were mailed a second reminder and a second copy of the questionnaire. During the week of January 22–26, 1968, telephone calls were made by local representatives of ASPA to all the members of the sample to encourage their response to the questionnaire.

Soon after the telephone campaign, over 50 percent of the questionnaires had been returned. However, by the end of the first week in February, the response rate had dropped to one or two questionnaires returned per day. Although 50 percent response was fairly typical for a national questionnaire, it did not satisfy our expectations. The contact network which had been set up had not been as effective as anticipated. And, due to the anonymity of the respondents, it was impossible to locate exactly those who had not responded. By checking postmarks, however, it was possible to select areas from which there had been less than a 50 percent response. By eliminating areas of a more than 50 percent response, the list of 623 personnel managers was reduced to 475. It was decided to telephone 220 of these who were in large urban areas. Three individuals were responsible for the phoning: the executive vice-president of ASPA in Berea, Ohio; the president of ASPA in St. Louis, Missouri; and the Cornell researchers in Ithaca, New York. The remaining 255 personnel managers resided in small towns and were sent telegrams on February 20, 1968. The phone calls and telegrams increased the response rate to over 60 percent by March 15, 1968 which was the previously decided upon cut-off date.

# APPENDICES

## Response rate

In gross figures, 419 of the sample of 623 male personnel managers returned completed questionnaires, a response rate of 66.2 percent. The literature on responses to mail questionnaires indicates that this was an extremely good response rate. For example, "Ferber reports that 0–50 percent are usual, and Goode and Hatt put the 'usual' number returned between 20 and 70 percent."[3] The only study comparable to the present one, cited by Robin (1965), obtained a 66 percent return rate.[4] However, that used a 10-page questionnaire while the present study's questionnaire was 16 pages.

The question could be raised: Are the 34 percent who did not respond different from the 66 percent who did respond? Robin reports that the findings on nonrespondents are unclear. Several authors "found significant differences in age, socioeconomic status, education and related characteristics between those who responded to their mail questionnaire and those who failed to do so."[5] Other researchers, however, "conclude from their research that there are no significant differences between responders and non-responders."[6] In surveying these contradictory findings, Robin concludes, "that differences between responders and non-responders seem to appear in investigations concerned with opinions, values, and psychological characteristics."[7] Since the current study is concerned with opinions and psychological characteristics, there is a problem with nonrespondents. The findings by Reuss (1943) gives some insight into what the differences between respondents and non-respondents in the present study might have been. Among other things, Reuss found those who responded to mail questionnaires were more intelligent, better educated, and more loyal to the institution sponsoring the questionnaire.[8] If that is true of the responders to the present study, then it reduces the ability to generalize. The population (ASPA) is already biased in the direction of the characteristics mentioned by Reuss and this bias may be increased by the nature of those who responded to the questionnaire.

The ideal solution to the problem of nonrespondents might be an effort to question them in order to determine whether they differ from the respondents. Because the present study was totally anonymous, this was not feasible. In order to get information on salary, work histories, opinions about others in the organization, and a personality score, anonymity was more important than solving the problem of nonrespondents in this study. The 34

---

[3]Stanley Robin, "A Procedure for Securing Returns to Mail Questionnaires," *Sociology and Social Research,* vol. 50, no. 1, 1965, p. 25.

[4]*ibid.,* p. 30.

[5]*ibid.,* p. 24.

[6]*ibid.,* p. 24.

[7]*ibid.,* p. 25.

[8]Carl F. Reuss, "Differences Between Persons Responding and Not Responding to a Mailed Questionnaire," *American Sociological Review,* vol. 8, August 1943, p. 438.

percent nonrespondents remains a limitation on the findings of the present study.

## Coding

The completed questionnaires were coded by members of the research team and several hired coders. In order to be sure that the coding was correct, each coded questionnaire was checked by another coder. In addition, every tenth code sheet, beginning with one randomly selected was checked to assess the error rate for the coding process. There was a total of 286 coded entries per questionnaire. The error rate was less than one per questionnaire.

## Reliability

Efforts to assess the reliability of the questionnaire proved difficult. Several local chapters of ASPA agreed to conduct test-retest reliability studies. What was needed was the completion of the questionnaire on two separate occasions by the same persons. The first three local chapters which tried this were able to supply a total of only 10 sets of questionnaires. Finally, a group of personnel administrators in the Pittsburgh area sent a set of 41 questionnaires which had been completed for the second time by the same respondents. The second questionnaire was filled out five weeks after the first. The reliability indices were generally high. On the *demographic data* the Pierson Product Moment Correlations ranged from .97 to 1.0. The items on *commitment to the organization* ranged from .83 to .93 with a mean of .87. The reliability on *commitment to the occupation* ranged from .83 to .94 with a mean of .89. The reliability on a *measure of authoritarianism,* included in the instrument, was .91. The reliability data are much the same for the *conflict material.* For example, on Case 1, the following were the reliability indices:

1–Experience with a case similar to 1 . . . . . . . . . . . . . . . . . . . . . . . . .94
2–Importance of Case 1 . . . . . . . . . . . . . . . . . . . . . . . . . . . . . . . . . . .88
3–Most Likely Action—Situation 1 . . . . . . . . . . . . . . . . . . . . . . . . .84
4–Most Likely Action—Situation 2 . . . . . . . . . . . . . . . . . . . . . . . . .87
5–Most Likely Action—Situation 3 . . . . . . . . . . . . . . . . . . . . . . . . .86
6–Most Likely Action—Situation 4 . . . . . . . . . . . . . . . . . . . . . . . . .85
7–Most Likely Action—Situation 5 . . . . . . . . . . . . . . . . . . . . . . . . .87
8–Most Likely Action—Situation 6 . . . . . . . . . . . . . . . . . . . . . . . . .85

The rankings of significant others in Case 1 had reliability scores ranging from .85 to .94 with a mean reliability of .90. The reliability indices for Case 1 are similar and, if anything, slightly higher.

## Validity

Assessing the validity of the questionnaire provided a somewhat more difficult problem. For some items there are actual behavioral data which can be compared to the questionnaire findings. These data are discussed at appropriate points in chapters of this book. For most of the questionnaire findings, however, there is no actual behavioral information. There is a means, though, of assessing the construct or trait validity of many of the questionnaire items. If the relationships, as they are hypothesized, are supported by the findings, then the items in the relationship can be treated as valid. This is similar to the approach used by Brim, *et al.* in *Personality and Decision Process*. They recognize, as we do, the following limitation on this type of validity: "Of course if the hypothesis is not confirmed, then the source of error is difficult to locate. Either the prediction is wrong or the measures. . . .are not relevant."[9] With this limitation in mind, it is reasonable to conclude that, to the extent the hypotheses are supported, the instrument is valid.

[9]Orville G. Brim, Jr., David C. Glass, David E. Lavin, and Norman Goodman, *Personality and Decision Process* (Stanford: Stanford University Press, 1962), p. 45.

# APPENDIX B

# Questionnaire

STUDY OF PERSONNEL OCCUPATIONS

CONDUCTED BY

SCHOOL OF INDUSTRIAL AND LABOR RELATIONS AT CORNELL

AND AMERICAN SOCIETY FOR PERSONNEL ADMINISTRATION

## PART I—SOME INFORMATION ABOUT YOURSELF

We don't want to know your name. However, we do need to know some things about you and your background.

The term personnel administration will be used in this questionnaire to cover all of the general personnel functions; included under this are industrial and labor relations.

Please return completed questionnaire to Professor Harrison Trice, School of Industrial and Labor Relations, Cornell University, Ithaca, New York 14850.

(1) Your age is ―― years.

(2) Sex: Male―― Female――

(3) What is your marital status? (Check one) Married ―― Single―― Widowed, Divorced, Separated ――

(4) How many children do you have? _____

(5) In what occupation has (did) your father spend the majority of his work life? (Check one)

Professional _____

Semi-Professional _____

Managers, Officials
and Proprietors _____

Clerical Workers _____

Sales Workers _____

Craftsmen and Foremen _____

Operatives and Kindred Workers _____

Private Household
and Service Workers _____

Laborers, Including Farm _____

(6) Please check the highest level of formal education completed by your *father*.

Grade School _____

Some High School _____

High School Graduate _____

Some College _____

College Graduate _____

Some work toward advanced degree _____

Advanced Degree _____

(7) Please check the highest level of formal education you have completed. (Where you have post-graduate work, also indicate your undergraduate degree and major. Be specific when indicating your major).

Grade School _____

Some High School _____

High School Graduate _____

Some College _____ Major _____

College Graduate _____ Type of degree _____ Major _____

Some work toward advanced degree _____ Major _____

Advanced degree _____ Type of degree _____ Major _____

97

(8) While you were still in school, did you plan to make your career in personnel administration? Yes——— No———

(9) In the course of your career in personnel administration have you been *encouraged* by any *one* individual?

Yes——— No——— Too many to specify———

    a) If yes, give the job title of the individual who encouraged you at the time he encouraged you.

    _____

    b) If yes, give the current job title of the individual who encouraged you.

    _____

(10) In the course of your career in personnel administration, has any *one* individual provided you with *actual* opportunities for advancement in the personnel field?

Yes——— No——— Too many to specify———

(11) In terms of your own career, what position would you like to reach in the next ten years?

_____

(12) Please list the professional associations (if any) to which you now belong. In the spaces following each name indicate the approximate length of membership and your estimate of how active you are in each organization. Indicate the degree of your activity in each association by circling the appropriate number in the farthest space opposite each name.

    0 = Inactive              2 = Moderately Active
    1 = Relatively Inactive   3 = Very Active

| Name (Give Full Title) | Length of Membership (In Yrs) | Activity |
| --- | --- | --- |
| _____ | _____ | 0  1  2  3 |
| _____ | _____ | 0  1  2  3 |
| _____ | _____ | 0  1  2  3 |
| _____ | _____ | 0  1  2  3 |

(13) Are the *majority* of the ethical standards by which the personnel administrator operates: (Check one)

_____ a) Determined by professional associations.

_____ b) Determined by the individual companies in which the personnel manager operates.

_____ c) Determined by the personnel manager himself without regard to professional associations or the company.

(14) If somehow you were forced to make a choice between staying in personnel administration in another company or staying in your present company, but not in personnel administration, which would you choose, assuming you couldn't do both?

(Check one)

_____ a) Stay in personnel administration in another company.

_____ b) Stay in your present company, but not in personnel administration.

_____ c) Wouldn't care since neither are particularly important to me.

99

(15) Suppose you were offered a job exactly like your present one in personnel administration, *but not in the same company*. Would you, under *each* of the following conditions, change companies? (Please indicate what you would do for each of the conditions listed on the left by putting a check mark in the desired box).

| | Yes, Definitely Change | Undecided | No, Definitely Not Change |
|---|---|---|---|
| With no increase in pay | | | |
| With a slight increase in pay | | | |
| With a large increase in pay | | | |
| With no more freedom | | | |
| With little more freedom | | | |
| With much more freedom | | | |
| With no more status | | | |

| | | | |
|---|---|---|---|
| With little more status | | | |
| With much more status | | | |
| With no more responsibility | | | |
| With little more responsibility | | | |
| With much more responsibility | | | |
| With no more opportunity to get ahead | | | |
| With reasonably more opportunity to get ahead | | | |
| With a great deal more opportunity to get ahead | | | |
| At another geographic location | | | |

For what other reason would you change (if any) _____

101

(16) Suppose you were offered a job comparable to your present one, *not in personnel administration*, although in the same company. Would you change occupations under each of the following conditions? (Please indicate what you would do for each of the conditions listed on the left by putting a check mark in the desired box).

|  | Yes, Definitely Change | Undecided | No, Definitely Not Change |
|---|---|---|---|
| With no increase in pay |  |  |  |
| With a slight increase in pay |  |  |  |
| With a large increase in pay |  |  |  |
| With no more freedom |  |  |  |
| With little more freedom |  |  |  |
| With much more freedom |  |  |  |
| With no more status |  |  |  |

With little more status

With much more status

With no more responsibility

With little more responsibility

With much more responsibility

With no more opportunity to get ahead

With reasonably more opportunity to get ahead

With a great deal more opportunity to get ahead

At another geographic location

For what other reason would you change (if any) _____

(17) In this question we are concerned with how you feel various groups influence personnel activities. Please rank the groups listed below in what you believe *actually* are their order of importance in determining your activities as a personnel administrator.

1 = Most Important
2 = Second Most Important
3 = Third Most Important
4 = Fourth Most Important
5 = Least Important

| Group | Rank |
|---|---|
| Yourself | ____ |
| Your subordinates in the Personnel Department | ____ |
| Other personnel people, both in your company and at other companies | ____ |
| Your immediate superior (e.g., the plant manager, President, etc.) | ____ |
| Other management officials at your location | ____ |

(18) Please again rank the various groups listed below. This time indicate what you feel their importance *should be* for a personnel administrator.

Please do not make comparisons with your previous answers. This is an opportunity to express how you feel other groups should influence your activities.

1 = Most Important
2 = Second Most Important
3 = Third Most Important
4 = Fourth Most Important
5 = Least Important

Yourself ...........................................................................

Your subordinates in the Personnel Department ........................

Other personnel people, both in your company and at other companies ......

Your immediate superior (e.g., the plant manager, President, etc.) ......

Other management officials at your location ......

(19) How many hours a week do you *actually* spend performing your job? —————

(20) Using the above figures as 100%, please allocate the percent of your total working time you feel you probably devote to each of the following activities. You may allocate no time (0%) to any of these, or you may add activities which you feel are excluded.

Supervising subordinates ..................................................... ——%

Planning personnel department activities ............................... ——%

Representing company to outside organizations (e.g., other companies, government) ...... ——%

Representing company to the union ......................................... ——%

Gathering information both inside and outside the organization ...... ——%

Providing information and advice for decision making by others in your organization ...... ——%

Making decisions on personnel matters for other departments in the company ...... ——%

Involved in professional functions, such as attending professional meetings ...... ——%

Other (Please specify) ......................................... ——%

Other (Please specify) ......................................... ——%

(21) How many hours a week *should* you spend performing your job? —————

(22) Using the above figure as 100%, please allocate the percent of your total working time you feel you *should* devote to each of the following activities. You may allocate no time (0%) to any of these, or you may add activities to which you feel time should be allocated.

Supervising subordinates ...................................................... ——%

Planning personnel department activities ...................................... ——%

Representing company to outside organizations (e.g., other companies, government) ...... ——%

Representing company to the union ............................................ ——%

Gathering information both inside and outside the organization ................. ——%

Providing information and advice for decision making by others in your organization ...... ——%

Making decisions on personnel matters for other departments in the company ...... ——%

Involved in professional functions, such as attending professional meetings ....... ——%

Other (Please specify) ....................................................... ——%

Other (Please specify) ....................................................... ——%

(23) We would like you in the following chart, to list your job history. Please start with your present job and work *in reverse order*, such that the last job listed in the chart should be the first job you held after you completed your formal schooling. Please be sure to list all changes in job title, changes in company, and changes in location. Please be sure to list military service when it occurred in your career.

| Major Responsibility | Years Job Held (from–to) | Major Product or Service of that Company | (Approx.) Number of Employees in Company | Job Location City & State | Ending Salary |
|---|---|---|---|---|---|
| 1. | | | | | |

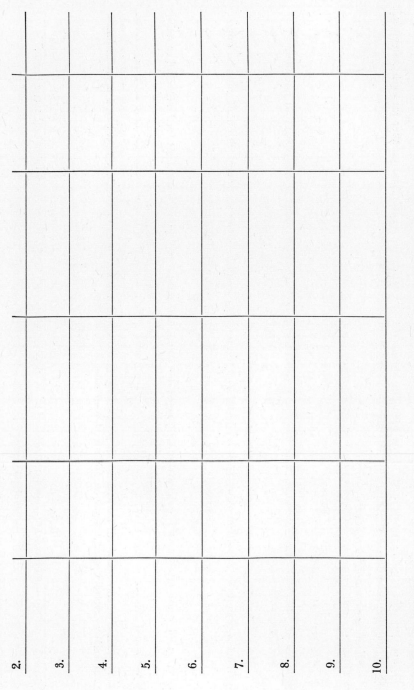

2.

3.

4.

5.

6.

7.

8.

9.

10.

(24) How many companies, in the course of your work career, have you worked for (excluding military organizations)? ———

## PART II—MORE ABOUT YOU

Please indicate your attitude toward each of the following statements by circling the appropriate number for each statement. There are no right or wrong answers for these statements, all we want is your opinion.

(1) Obedience and respect for authority are the most important virtues children should learn.

Strongly Agree   1   2   3   4   5   6   7   Strongly Disagree

(2) Every person should have complete faith in some supernatural power whose decisions he obeys without question.

Strongly Agree   1   2   3   4   5   6   7   Strongly Disagree

(3) When a person has a problem or worry, it is best for him not to think about it, but to keep busy with more cheerful things.

Strongly Agree   1   2   3   4   5   6   7   Strongly Disagree

(4) What the youth needs most is strict discipline, rugged determination, and the will to work and fight for family and country.

Strongly Agree   1   2   3   4   5   6   7   Strongly Disagree

(5) Nowadays when so many different kinds of people move around and mix together so much, a person has to protect himself especially carefully against catching an infection or disease from them.

Strongly Agree   1   2   3   4   5   6   7   Strongly Disagree

(6) Young people sometimes get rebellious ideas, but as they grow up they ought to get over them and settle down.

Strongly Agree   1   2   3   4   5   6   7   Strongly Disagree

(7) People can be divided into two distinct classes: the weak and the strong.

Strongly Agree  1  2  3  4  5  6  7  Strongly Disagree

(8) There is hardly anything lower than a person who does not feel a great love, gratitude, and respect for his parents.

Strongly Agree  1  2  3  4  5  6  7  Strongly Disagree

(9) Someday it will probably be shown that astrology can explain a lot of things.

Strongly Agree  1  2  3  4  5  6  7  Strongly Disagree

(10) Nowadays more and more people are prying into matters that should remain personal and private.

Strongly Agree  1  2  3  4  5  6  7  Strongly Disagree

(11) Most of our social problems would be solved if we could somehow get rid of the immoral, crooked, and feeble-minded people.

Strongly Agree  1  2  3  4  5  6  7  Strongly Disagree

(12) If people would talk less and work more, everybody would be better off.

Strongly Agree  1  2  3  4  5  6  7  Strongly Disagree

(13) No sane, normal decent person could ever think of hurting a close friend or relative.

Strongly Agree  1  2  3  4  5  6  7  Strongly Disagree

## PART III — HOW WOULD YOU ACT IN A GIVEN SITUATION

In this section we are interested in comparing how personnel managers act in hypothetical situations. Would you please tell us how you would act if these were actual situations confronting you in your job.

We are trying to discover something about personnel administrators which will be of great interest and usefulness to them in the future. For that reason *please read the instructions very carefully.*

There are five significant figures in the following case:

1) Yourself

2) The manager of the accounting department

3) The man immediately above you in the personnel department

4) The top company official at your location

5) Your immediate subordinate whose knowledge would be relevant to this situation

The case is as follows:

Several weeks ago a terrible storm hit your area. Because of the storm a number of the employees at your location were unable to get to work. The employees involved were not in a union. This is the first time such a situation has occurred at your location and there is no policy or precedent on handling such an issue. You have thought over the situation and decided that there are good arguments for both paying and not paying the employees for time lost. Although you are now undecided you have sought *advice* from significant figures in your organization. Your recommendation will be based *solely* on the advice you receive in each case.

It must be stressed that *YOUR OWN OPINION ON THIS ISSUE SHOULD HAVE NO INFLUENCE ON YOUR RECOMMENDATION. Your recommendation should be based only on the information in the above case and in each of the 6 situations based on this case, which are on the following 2 pages.*

In each of the following situations one of the above significant figures is going to advise you (no one will order you) to do one thing about pay for time lost due to the storm, while the other is going to want you to do exactly the opposite. In each case you cannot do both, so we want you to decide, in each instance, what you would do.

Each instance is separate from the others and your decision in one should not affect your decision in any of the others. You should act as if the people in this case are the actual people in your organization. If one or more of the positions does not exist at your location we would like you to act as if they actually do exist.

*111*

Before we proceed, we would like you to tell us about the case described above:

a) Have you ever had any actual experience with a case like this? Yes_____ No_____

b) Whether or not you have had experience with a similar situation, how important is this kind of a situation to you?

Unimportant _____:_____:_____:_____:_____ Very Important
                 1      2      3      4      5

c) Do you actually have contact with each of the significant figures in this case? (Please check yes or no for each.)

The manager of the accounting department Yes_____ No_____

The man immediately above you in the personnel department Yes_____ No_____

The top company official at your location Yes_____ No_____

Your immediate subordinate whose knowledge would be relevant to this situation Yes_____ No_____

Please put a (1) next to the action you would be *most* likely to take. Put a (2) next to the action you would be *least* likely to take.

1 = most likely action
2 = least likely action

1) The man immediately above you in the personnel department is in favor of paying for the time lost, but the top company official at your location is opposed.

_____ Recommend pay for the time lost

_____ Do not recommend pay for the time lost

_____ Talk to the two parties and attempt to resolve their differences

_____ Listen to both but make your own recommendation

_____ Hold your recommendation in abeyance

2) The manager of the accounting department is in favor of paying for the time lost, but the man immediately above you in the personnel department is opposed.

_____ Do not recommend pay for the time lost

_____ Talk to the two parties and attempt to resolve their differences

_____ Listen to both but make your own recommendation

_____ Hold your recommendation in abeyance

_____ Recommend pay for the time lost

*113*

Reminder: (1) = most likely; (2) = least likely

3) The top company official at your location is in favor of paying for the time lost, but the manager of the accounting department is opposed.

___ Talk to the two parties and attempt to resolve their differences

___ Listen to both but make your own recommendation

___ Hold your recommendation in abeyance

___ Recommend pay for the time lost

___ Do not recommend pay for the time lost

4) The manager of the accounting department is in favor of paying for the time lost, but your immediate subordinate whose knowledge would be relevant to this situation is opposed.

___ Listen to both but make your own recommendation

___ Hold your recommendation in abeyance

___ Recommend pay for the time lost

___ Do not recommend pay for the time lost

___ Talk to the two parties and attempt to resolve their differences

5) Your immediate subordinate is in favor of paying for the time lost, but the top company official at your location is opposed.

_____ Hold your recommendation in abeyance

_____ Recommend pay for the time lost

_____ Do not recommend pay for the time lost

_____ Talk to the two parties and attempt to resolve their differences

_____ Listen to both but make your own recommendation

6) Your immediate subordinate is in favor of paying for the time lost, but the man immediately above you in the personnel department is opposed.

_____ Recommend pay for the time lost

_____ Do not recommend pay for the time lost

_____ Talk to the two parties and attempt to resolve their differences

_____ Listen to both but make your own recommendation

_____ Hold your recommendation in abeyance

115

Now that you have made these choices of action, we would like you to rank the positions you had to deal with in the above situations. We would like you to rank each of the four positions (the manager of the accounting department, the man immediately above you in the personnel department, your immediate subordinate, whose knowledge would be relevant to this situation, and the top company official at your location) on five factors. If one or more of the positions does not exist at your location, we would like you to act as if they actually do exist.

For each of the five factors put a (1) next to the man who ranks highest (e.g. has the most) on that factor, a (2) next to the second highest, a (3) next to the third highest, and a (4) next to the lowest on that factor. Please be sure *each* blank is filled.

1) Please rank the following positions on the right they have, based on formal organizational rules, to expect you to follow their advice on this issue:

—— The manager of the accounting department

—— The man immediately above you in the personnel department

—— The top company official at your location

—— Your immediate subordinate whose knowledge would be relevant to this situation

2) Please rank the following positions on the ability they have to actually see what action you take, or find out about it later:

—— The manager of the accounting department

—— The man immediately above you in the personnel department

—— The top company official at your location

—— Your immediate subordinate whose knowledge would be relevant to this situation

3) Please rank the following positions on the amount of knowledge they have on this type of issue:

_____ The manager of the accounting department

_____ The man immediately above you in the personnel department

_____ The top company official at your location

_____ Your immediate subordinate whose knowledge would be relevant to this situation

4) Please rank the following positions in terms of how friendly you are with each of them:

_____ The manager of the accounting department

_____ The man immediately above you in the personnel department

_____ The top company official at your location

_____ Your immediate subordinate whose knowledge would be relevant to this situation

5) Please rank the following positions on their ability to compel you to follow their advice:

_____ The manager of the accounting department

_____ The man immediately above you in the personnel department

_____ The top company official at your location

_____ Your immediate subordinate whose knowledge would be relevant to this situation

We would like you to tell us how you would behave in another case. It is as follows:

An outside consultant was hired some months ago by your company to study the personnel department. He has just submitted his report and, among other things, it recommends several changes in the duties assigned to you. You see both merits and failings in the suggested changes. On the whole, therefore, you are undecided on whether the company should accept the recommendations for change. Although you are now undecided you have been told that you must make a recommendation. Since you are undecided you have sought *advice* from significant figures in your organization. Your decision will be based *solely* on the advice you receive in each case.

Once again it must be stressed that *YOUR OWN OPINION ON THIS ISSUE SHOULD HAVE NO INFLUENCE ON YOUR RECOMMENDATION*. Your recommendation should be based *only* on the information in the above case and in each of the 6 situations based on this case, which are on the following 2 pages.

As before, there are five significant figures in this case:

1) Yourself

2) The manager of the accounting department

3) The man immediately above you in the personnel department

4) The top company official at your location

5) Your immediate subordinate whose knowledge would be relevant to this situation

In each of the following situations one of the above is going to advise you (no one will order you) about making changes in your job, while the other is going to want you to do exactly the opposite. In each situation you cannot do both, so we want you to decide what you would do. Each situation is separate from the others and your decision in one should not affect your decision in any of the others.

You should act as if the people in this case are the actual people in your organization. If one or more of the positions does not exist at your location we would like you to act as if they actually do exist.

Before we proceed, we would like you to answer questions about the situation described above:

a) Have you ever had any experience with a situation like this?  Yes_____  No_____

b) How important is this kind of a situation to you?

Unimportant _____:_____:_____:_____:_____ : Very Important
             1    2    3    4    5

c) Do you actually have contact with each of the significant figures in this case? (Please check yes or no for each.)

The manager of the accounting department  Yes_____  No_____

The man immediately above you in the personnel department  Yes_____  No_____

The top company official at your location  Yes_____  No_____

Your immediate subordinate whose knowledge would be relevant to this situation  Yes_____  No_____

Please put a (1) next to the action you would be *most* likely to take. Put a (2) next to the action you would be *least* likely to take.

    1 = most likely action
    2 = least likely action

1) The man immediately above you in the personnel department is in favor of the changes, but the top company official at your location is opposed.

_____ Recommend the changes

_____ Do not recommend the changes

_____ Talk to the two parties and attempt to resolve their differences

_____ Listen to both but make your own recommendation

_____ Hold your recommendation in abeyance

2) The manager of the accounting department is in favor of the changes, but the man immediately above you in the personnel department is opposed.

_____ Do not recommend the changes

_____ Talk to the two parties and attempt to resolve their differences

_____ Listen to both but make your own recommendation

_____ Hold your recommendation in abeyance

_____ Recommend the changes

Reminder: (1) = most likely   (2) = least likely

3) The top company official at your location is in favor of the changes, but the manager of the accounting department is opposed.

_____ Talk to the two parties and attempt to resolve their differences

_____ Listen to both but make your own recommendation

_____ Hold your recommendation in abeyance

_____ Recommend the changes

_____ Do not recommend the changes

4) The manager of the accounting department is in favor of the changes, but your immediate subordinate whose knowledge would be relevant to this situation, is opposed.

_____ Listen to both but make your own recommendation

_____ Hold your recommendation in abeyance

_____ Recommend the changes

_____ Do not recommend the changes

_____ Talk to the two parties and attempt to resolve their differences

122

5) Your immediate subordinate whose knowledge would be relevant to this situation is in favor of the changes, but the top company official at your location is opposed.

———— Hold your recommendation in abeyance

———— Recommend the changes

———— Do not recommend the changes

———— Talk to the two parties and attempt to resolve their differences

———— Listen to both but make your own recommendation

6) Your immediate subordinate whose knowledge would be relevant to this situation is in favor of the changes, but the man immediately above you in the personnel department is opposed.

———— Recommend the changes

———— Do not recommend the changes

———— Talk to the two parties and attempt to resolve their differences

———— Listen to both but make your own recommendation

———— Hold your recommendation in abeyance

Now that you have made these choices of action, we would like you to rank the positions you had to deal with in this second situation. We would like you to rank each of the four positions (the manager of the accounting department, the man immediately above you in the personnel department, your immediate subordinate whose knowledge would be relevant to this situation, and the top company official at your location) on five factors. If one or more of the positions does not exist at your location, we would like you to act as if they actually do exist.

For each of the five factors put a (1) next to the man who ranks highest (e.g. has the most) on that factor, a (2) next to the second highest, a (3) next to the third highest, and a (4) next to the lowest on that factor. Please be sure *each* blank is filled.

1) Please rank the following positions on the right they have, based on formal organizational rules, to expect you to follow their advice on this issue:

_____ The manager of the accounting department

_____ The man immediately above you in the personnel department

_____ The top company official at your location

_____ Your immediate subordinate whose knowledge would be relevant to this situation

2) Please rank the following positions on the ability they have to actually see what action you take, or find out about it later:

_____ The manager of the accounting department

_____ The man immediately above you in the personnel department

_____ The top company official at your location

_____ Your immediate subordinate whose knowledge would be relevant to this situation

124

3) Please rank the following positions on the amount of knowledge they have on this type of issue:

_____ The manager of the accounting department

_____ The man immediately above you in the personnel department

_____ The top company official at your location

_____ Your immediate subordinate whose knowledge would be relevant to this situation

4) Please rank the following positions in terms of how friendly you are with each of them:

_____ The manager of the accounting department

_____ The man immediately above you in the personnel department

_____ The top company official at your location

_____ Your immediate subordinate whose knowledge would be relevant to this situation

5) Please rank the following positions on their ability to compel you to follow their advice:

_____ The manager of the accounting department

_____ The man immediately above you in the personnel department

_____ The top company official at your location

_____ Your immediate subordinate whose knowledge would be relevant to this situation

125

# APPENDIX C

# Interview Schedule

I. *Demographic Data*

    A. *Personal*

        1. What is your education and work experience?
          a. Major, if college
          b. School and year of graduation
          c. Work experience in line or staff
          d. Age

    B. *Subordinates*

        1. What is the academic background and work experience of your subordinates?
          a. Schooling
          b. Work experience
          c. Age

    C. *Organizational*

        1. Product or service
        2. Size of company
        3. Organizational structure

II. *Superior-Subordinate Conflict*

    A. Please describe for me, in as much detail as possible, a situation in which you and one of your subordinates have held dissenting views on an issue related to the work activity.

        1. What was the issue
        2. How did it develop
        3. Who was involved

*126*

4. What positions were taken, why
5. What actions were taken toward solution
6. Who had final say, why
7. What were alternative solutions
8. What was the outcome after solution was implemented

III. *Role Conflict*

A. Now that you have described a conflictive situation with subordinates, please tell me one in which you have had to intervene and present a solution to conflicting views between two other persons in the organization.

1. What was the issue
2. How did it develop
3. Who was involved
4. What were the positions taken, why
5. What actions were taken toward solution
6. Who had the final say, why
7. What were the alternative solutions
8. What was final outcome after the solution was implemented

IV. *Situations Faced (Conflictive)*

A. Please describe now the third type of conflictive situation. That is, one in which you and somebody else have dissented in your views on a given issue.

1. What was the issue
2. How did it develop
3. Who was involved
4. What were the positions taken, why
5. What actions were taken toward solution
6. Who had the final say, why
7. What were the alternative solutions
8. What was the final outcome

3